A Comprehensive Guide

For Listing

A Building In

The National Register

Of Historic Places

By

Gail Greenberg

WITHDRAWN

Highland Township Library
205 W. Livingston, P.O. Box 277
Highland, Michigan 48357
887-2218

Mon-Thurs 10-8
Fri-Sat   10-5
Sunday   Closed

Lucid Press
Sausalito, California
1996

To Bob
for his patience and understanding of my
time spent at the computer instead of with him

A Comprehensive Guide to
Listing a Building in the
National Register of Historic Places

© 1996 Gail Greenberg. All Rights Reserved
No portion of this book may be reproduced or
used in any form, or by any means, without
written permission of the publishers.

Printed in the United States of America

Library of Congress Cataloging-in-Publication Data

National Register of Historic Places
1. Handbook-Manual
E159.G69   1996
363. 6' 9'—dc20   95-53095
                                                  CIP
ISBN 0-9646184-0-0

Cover Illustration by Bob Pagett from his drawing of the
"Jack London House," Sausalito, California

Copy Editor: A Ranney Johnson

Published by Lucid Press
10 Liberty Ship Way
Sausalito, California 94965

10 9 8 7 6 5 4 3 2 1

Foreword

During the time spent in my present position as Executive Director of the Camden County (NJ) Cultural and Heritage Commission (and it astounds me to realize that it has been more than 22 years!) as well as in teaching and a study of the law, I have been continually amazed at the advantages offered by, and the frustrations of dealing with, government regulations. It is a fact that there are many, many benefits offered us in a myriad of ways from our national, state and local governments. However, in our attempts to realize such gains, we often become bewildered and eventually abandon our goals because of the obtuseness of government-issued instructions and forms.

The purpose of this book is to provide more comprehensive answers to the many requests I have received for assistance in making application for listing in the State and National Registers of Historic Places. Many other authorities in this field of historic preservation and research, have confirmed that they, too, get lost in the maze of complicated language and instructions.

If you use the directions specified in this volume, your goal of having your building enrolled onto the official State and Federal lists of buildings significant to American history, architecture, archaeology, engineering or culture will be within reach. Everything you need is here in simplified form.

Gail Greenberg

Moorestown, New Jersey
January 30, 1996

About the Author

Historian Gail Greenberg, recipient of the New Jersey Historical Commission's 1994 "Local Historian's Award of Distinction" makes her home in Moorestown, New Jersey. She is President of the Association of New Jersey County Cultural and Historic Agencies, the Executive Director of the Camden County (NJ) Cultural and Heritage Commission, Historian of Camden County and its Historic Preservation Professional. In 1995 she was appointed by New Jersey Governor Christine Todd Whitman to a new State Task Force on New Jersey History which will study the ways government and private agencies deliver historical services to the public. This book is the result of the many requests she has had for assistance in making application to list a building in the National Register of Historic Places.

Contents

INTRODUCTION

WHAT IS THE NATIONAL REGISTER

OF HISTORIC PLACES (NRHP) ?

The National Register of Historic Places (NRHP) is the nation's official list of properties that are significant in American history, architecture, archaeology, engineering or culture.

The Register is composed of districts, sites, buildings, structures and objects and is maintained by the National Park Service, Department of the Interior, Washington, DC. Additionally, each state maintains a State Register of Historic Places (SRHP). Nominations are processed through the SRHP before placement on the NRHP.

WHAT ARE THE BENEFITS OF LISTING?

Listing in the NRHP conveys recognition of the property's historic importance and confers a certain prestige to it. Also, there are a number of protections and benefits available for properties that are registered.

For example, listing in the NRHP and SRHP guarantees that public projects, such as road-widening, which might encroach upon or adversely affect the character of the historic structure, will be subject to review and comment in accordance with Section 106 of the National Historic Preservation Act of 1966.

An encroachment is an undertaking that will have a negative impact on a registered property. It does not include routine maintenance, which is not subject to review. Listing in the SRHP gives the same protection for properties that might be encroached upon by State, County or Municipal undertakings; in such cases, a similar State-level review takes place.

Owners of properties listed in the NRHP may be eligible for a 20% investment tax credit for substantial rehabilitation of income-producing, certified historic structures such as commercial, industrial or rental residential buildings.

Federal tax deductions also are available for charitable contributions of easements on historically important land areas or structures. When Federal and/or State historic preservation funds are available in the form of grants or low-interest loans, NRHP status is required.

There are no disadvantages to listing a qualified property since owners of listed private properties are free to maintain, manage or dispose of their property as they choose (within the limits of municipal zoning codes) provided that no Federal monies are involved. The public does not automatically have the right to visit a listed property. And the owner's ability to sell or lease the land or house to any buyer is unrestricted.

The expenses of listing a property are small if the owner does the necessary research and prepares the application forms. Costs involved include the purchase of a United States Geological Survey Map; travel to the county seat and local historical societies for research, and the costs of photocopying, film and film-processing. There is no application fee.

Now that you understand what the National Register of Historic Places means, and the benefits listing can bring to the owner of an historic house, let us consider on what basis your house can be certified as "historic."

CHAPTER ONE

WHAT ARE THE CRITERIA FOR APPLICATION?

Often, when my telephone rings, it is one of many inquiries which begins, "My house is historic because it is 100 years old and I want information on how to have it listed on the National Register of Historic Places (NRHP)."

Age is not the most important factor in determining whether a building is "historic." As a matter of fact, properties listed in the NRHP only need be at least fifty years old, but they must have historical or architectural significance and retain their original character or integrity.

This means that the location, design, setting, materials, workmanship, feeling and associations of the building must have survived. The physical characteristics that existed during the property's period of importance should remain mostly unaltered. All of the above qualities need not be present for eligibility, as long as a sense of place and time remains.

To be eligible for nomination your property must be important under one of four yardsticks known as **Criterions.** Please bear this in mind when doing research and presenting your case. Both the State and Federal lists recognize districts, sites, structures, buildings and objects that maintain integrity of location, design, setting, materials, workmanship, feeling and association and the following Criterions:

> **Criterion A:** that is associated with an important event or series of events that have made a significant contribution to the broad patterns of American History.
> *Significance under this criterion means that the historic event/events must have occurred on/in the property.*

Criterion B: that is associated with an important individual who was significant in our past.
Significance under this criterion means that the important individual should have lived in, or worked on the property during the period in which the person attained significance.

Criterion C: that embodies the distinctive characteristics of an architectural type, period, or method of construction. It may represent the work of a master or possess high artistic value.

Criterion D: that has yielded, or may be likely to yield, information important in prehistory or history.

OTHER CONSIDERATIONS

There are some categories of properties that *usually* are not considered eligible for nomination. They include:

* cemeteries, birthplaces and graves of historical figures,
* properties owned by religious institutions or used for religious purposes,
* structures that have been moved from their original locations; that have been rebuilt or are primarily commemorative in nature and,
* properties less than 50 years old.

Exceptions to the above are properties that are essential parts of districts that meet the criteria or if they fall into one of the following categories:

a. A religious property that has primary significance because of architectural/ artistic distinction or historical importance.
Example: The First Presbyterian Church, Cottage Grove, Oregon is a notable example of the Northwest style of architecture designed by Italian-born architect, Pietro Belluschi who played a role in developing the style.

4

b. A building removed from its original location but which is significant primarily for its architecture or is the surviving structure most importantly associated with an historic person or event.
Example: the Alexander Young Cabin, Washington, Iowa, built of logs in 1840 by a pioneer settler, Alexander Young, and moved from its original site in 1912.

c. A birthplace or grave of an historical figure of outstanding importance *if* there is no other appropriate site or building directly associated with that person's productive life.
Example: the Alice Paul House, Mount Laurel, New Jersey, birthplace of the suffragist most responsible for the Equal Rights Amendment.

d. A cemetery that derives its primary significance from graves of persons of great importance; from age; from distinctive design features, or from association with historic events.
Example: Christ Church Burial Ground, Philadelphia, Pennsylvania, which contains the graves of many early Americans, including Benjamin Franklin and noted physician, Philip Syng Physick.

e. A reconstructed building when accurately executed in a suitable environment and presented in a dignified manner as part of a restoration master plan, *and* when no other building or structure with the same association has survived.
Example: the central wing of The Old Barracks, Trenton, New Jersey. Built as a barracks during the French & Indian Wars, it housed Hessian, English and American soldiers during the American Revolution.

f. A property primarily commemorative in intent if design, age, tradition or symbolic value has given it its own historical signficance.
Example: the Ames Monument, near Sherman, Wyoming, a 60 foot high granite pyramid designed by architect, Henry Hobson Richardson, with sculptures by Augustus Saint-Gaudens, commemorating the role of the Ames brothers in building the Union Pacific Railroad.

The left portion of this New Jersey brick Quaker farmstead, the
Ebenezer Hopkins House, was built c.1757.
The wing on the right is a 20th Century
reincarnation of a late1700s addition

g. A property achieving significance *within* the past fifty years *if* it is of exceptional importance.
Example: two properties in Columbus, Ohio associated with folk artist Elijah Pierce were listed in the NRHP even though, at the time Mr. Pierce was still alive and had achieved significance only within the prior 50 years. It was shown that Pierce's folk art was viewed as extremely important and the buildings (his residence and gallery) were the only existing properties associated with the artist and they had been so for almost 40 years.

By now you should have some idea about the area of significance on which you will base your research and nomination. So, let's get started by organizing the information you will need in order to fill out the nomination form.

CHAPTER TWO

GETTING STARTED

In order to ensure a successful nomination your research must be thorough and accurate. You must discover what information is required in order to present your case for having the property listed as historic. Once this is done, it is not difficult to prepare a plan which will lead you to the answers.

Tools You Will Need

Before beginning your research be sure to contact the State Historic Preservation Officer (SHPO) in the state where the property is located and request the appropriate nomination forms and instructions as well as the state's guidelines for nominating properties to the NRHP. Ask if your property has already been documented and request a copy of the documentation. The SHPO also can tell you if there is a local preservation office in your community which you should contact for assistance.

You will be required to submit a 7.5 or 15 minute series United States Geological Survey (USGS) Map so that you can locate your property within a city or other geographical area. These are obtainable at map supply outlets for under $5.00. If there is no USGS map for your area, a State highway map may be used. Do not submit fragments or copies of any map; do not use adhesive labels or write in ink on the map. Using pencil only, place an X where the historic structure is located. In the margin of the map write the name of the structure, municipality, county and state of location, block and lot number and size of land area.

At least two sets of clear, detailed black and white photographs of the property will be required with the nomination form. They should be of high quality, on double or medium weight paper with a standard finish--either matte, glossy or satin, preferably 8 x 10 inches in size but a minimum of 3 1/2 inches x 5 inches will be accepted. Do not mount, or staple or glue them to the forms. Do label them with a soft lead pencil on the back or use a continuation sheet. The following information should be included:

1. Name of property
2. County and state where property is located
3. Name of photographer (including yourself)
4. Date of photograph
5. Location of original negative
6. Description of view indicating direction camera is facing. Example: " Northeast facade of house, facing south"
7. Photograph number.

If you are using a continuation sheet, each photo should be labeled with item numbers 1, 2 and 7 above. The remaining information can be listed on the sheet. Information common to all photographs may be listed once with a statement that it "applies to all photographs".

The number of views you provide depends on the size and complexity of the property. Submit as many as are necessary to show the condition and important aspects of the property. It also is useful to send prints or photocopies of historic photographs of the property to aid in documenting the building or to prove that it retains its integrity despite alterations. Make sure these also are labeled with name of property, county and state and date of photograph. If the exact date is not known, approximate it as closely as possible and add "circa" to the date. *Example:* " circa 1792."

Send enough views to show the main facades as well as the property's setting; any additions, or alterations also should be visible. Be sure to include views of interiors, landscaping, and unusual details, etc. if the property's significance is based on them.

Questions That Must Be Answered

You really cannot begin to gather the facts unless you know the questions that must be answered. The answers also will help you focus on the area of significance or "criterion" under which the house should be nominated to the NRHP.
The questions are:

1. What is the historic name of the house?

This is what the property was called during the time it was associated with an important event or persons or took on its significant physical characteristics. It might, for instance, be the name of the original owner, (*The Peter Mott House*), or its original use (*The Benjamin Cooper Ferry House*) or a nickname (*Cooper's Folly*). If the property does not have an historic name you will be able to choose a "preferred" name to be used for NRHP documents and publications, but you will have to explain why it is preferred.

2. How many buildings, structures or other resources are part of the property?

Most often the property is composed of a single building; however, as in the case of a farmstead, the grounds might also contain more than one homestead, perhaps an ice house, a smoke house, barn and silo, etc.

3. What is the location, address and name of present owner?

4. What is the date or period of construction of the building or buildings and when they attained their present form?

5. What is the name of the architect, designer or chief carpenter?

What changes or additions have been made over time? Who were the architects involved and the dates of their activities? How have these changes affected the architectural integrity of the house? The fact that a building has changed over time will not necessarily make it ineligible for nomination. However, it should retain sufficient integrity (historic fabric) to convey its association with the architecture, historic events or noted personages on which you are basing its significance.

6. What are the names of the original and subsequent owners?

This will provide you with a Chain of Title which should be submitted with the nomination form. Did the owners make any important contributions to history? (See Chapter Three for information on how to do a deed search.)

7. What was the property's original use?

How is it used today? Has it been moved? Why? When? How? How has the move affected the integrity of the property?

8. What historical events are associated with the house?

When did this association take place? This information should be provided even if it is not the basis for nomination. *For example*, while you may nominate the building because it was designed by William Strickland, if it was pressed into use as a field hospital during the Revolutionary War, this fact should be provided as more evidence of the importance of the structure.

9. What is the current condition of the property, its grounds and setting?

What are the property's boundaries? Its size? Where is it located on a USGS (United States Geological Service) map?

10. In what area or areas of history is the property significant i.e., which of the National Register Criteria apply to it ?

11. Are there any archaeological artifacts on the property? Have they been evaluated? To what period do they relate?

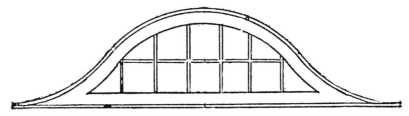

The eyebrow window was a small dormer set in low-pitched roofs to let in light. Wilson Eyre, Jr. used it in his design of the Charles Potter House c. 1885, Chestnut Hill, PA.

Chapter Three

RESEARCHING THE HISTORY OF A HOUSE

You must take the time to acquire intimate knowledge of the house, its features, the people who lived in it and the events that took place there.

This chapter provides a basic primer for techniques on how to collect information you will need to make a comprehensive and convincing case for the status of your property. Since walls can't talk, it is up to you to find and sift through all the sources of information available to you that will provide clues about the past history of your property.

Using The Physical Evidence

Take a careful walk around the exterior of the property. Make notes of the structure's setting, the arrangement of the building on the grounds and the neighborhood. I find it helpful to draw a rough sketch of the building and the grounds so that later, when I am writing the narrative description, I have a source of information that does not depend upon my memory.

Is the building in a residential setting? Is it located in an industrial park or shopping center? Is it on the edge of the industrial park? Near a major Interstate Highway or on a small, one-lane country road? Is it a single, detached unit or one of a duplex or part of a row of buildings? What is its relationship to the surroundings?

What is the overall shape of the structure? Is it a center hall "Colonial" with rooms on each side of a central entry, or is it a side entry Federal-style building with all rooms emanating from a side hall?

What is the number of stories in the house? What is the arrangement, number and design of the windows? Are they double hung, or casement windows? How many panes are in each window? Double hung windows described as "six over six" (6/6) have six panes in each of its two halves. If there are five windows or door openings on the first floor and the same number of openings on the second floor placed exactly above those on the first floor, the structure can be described as a "five bay house with balanced fenestration."

What is the shape of the roof? If it is gabled, it has a triangular-shaped, double sloping roof; if a hip roof, it has a somewhat square shape caused by the roof sloping upward from all four sides of the building, rather than on just two sides as in the gable roof; if a shed roof, it has only one sloping plane with the upper end butting against the wall of the house.

Now, slowly scrutinize the house. Note the number and location of porches, windows, doors, chimneys, dormers and any important decorative features such as bargeboards, pilasters, brackets, columns, cornices, turrets, oriels, dentilations. Are there any window and door ornamentations, shutters, shutter-dogs, etc.? These are the distinctive elements which set houses apart and help to date them.

(Note: Architectural terms should be used in the nomination. It is essential that you obtain one of the many excellent handbooks that describe building styles and contain a glossary of terms. See Appendix for recommended readings.)

Observe the location of other buildings or structures on the property and describe them. Do they appear to be the same age as the main building? Are they older? Are they newer? Also note the location of roads and landscape features including unusual trees and shrubs or an old herb garden, etc.

Record the visible materials that describe the foundation and walls; the roof, the chimney (if one exists), porches, lintels, cornices and other decorative elements. Choose from the Data Categories for Materials List on Page 52 the word that best depicts the elements that are *visible* to your eyes.

After you have completed a comprehensive description of the exterior of the house, continue in an organized manner, with a description of the inside. Begin in the basement. Describe the walls, foundation and floor. Locate windows, bulkheads and stairs.

Inspect beams and joists; describe how they are joined together. Are they nailed, or do they have mortise-and-tenon joints? Examine and describe any nails that may be visible. Are saw marks visible? Describe them; are they circular? Machine cut? Hand sawn?

Continue your inspection of the house, noting the overall floor plan and the dimensions of each room. Be sure to describe any outstanding features, including the flooring, chair rails, wainscoting, mantels, fireplace surrounds, and wall surfaces. If alterations have been made include the description at the appropriate location. *For example*, "In 1812 an addition was made to the north side of the building, approximately 21 feet long by 8 feet wide. This became a kitchen and servants' sleeping area but now is used as a dining room and butler's pantry. However, the windows and floor boards are original."

The characteristics and architectural details you have noted in your inspection of the house will aid in the dating process and the information will form the basis of the architectural description portion of the nomination form.

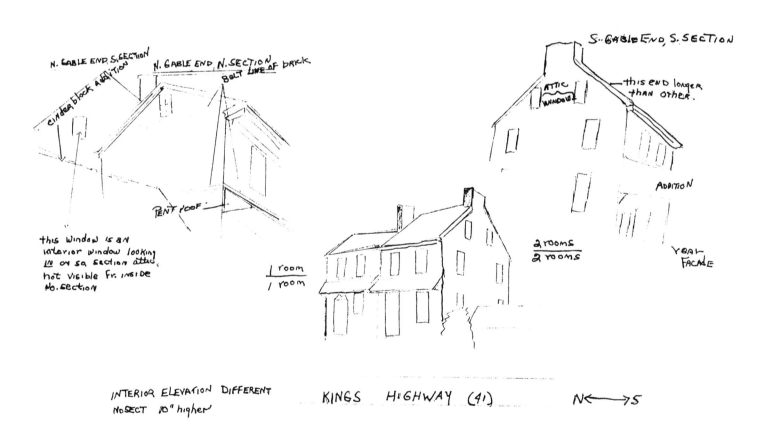

DOCUMENTARY SOURCES

County and Local Histories are the best basic sources of information on events, people, historic structures, dates, biographies and other data of community importance. These publications are found in the reference section of your local or regional library and historical society. They offer good grounding in the chronology and traditions of your locale which are important to know before deciding on the applicable National Register criteria.

Old City Directories contain, in alphabetical order, the names, addresses, occupations, and sometimes the race of residents. Businesses, physicians, merchants, contractors, government officials, banks and restaurants often are listed in a separate advertising or classified section. I often have discovered the names of children, spouses and siblings and their addresses and occupations by perusing these listings. Indications of race and religion can help to uncover old ethnic neighborhoods. These resources may be found in local and regional libraries; college and university libraries, and historical societies.

Atlases, Historic Maps, Plats, Developers' Plans and Aerial Photographs also are to be found in local libraries and historical societies. These provide information on boundaries, land uses, neighboring buildings and old street names. Two publishers, Sanborn and Baist, specialized in printing maps used for insurance purposes. These provide information on whether a lot was developed, when a house was built, its size and building material, the owner or developer, accessways, outbuildings and street names.

The Library of Congress, Geography and Map Division, Washington, DC 20540 has a Sanborn Map collection and thousands of 19th and 20th Century county and municipal maps. When writing for the availability of maps be sure to give the name of your state, county and municipality.

Deeds, Wills, Tax, Probate, Surrogate and Estate Records such as Inventories, Appraisals and Returns are located in county courthouses and state archives. Contact the local source first for information on whereabouts.

Each of the 21 counties in New Jersey has its own offices of Surrogate, Clerk and Register of Deeds usually found at the county courthouse or administration building in the county seat. Most other states have a similar arrangement which can be determined by calling the county courthouse and asking where such records are maintained.

To undertake a deed search it is helpful to begin by locating the most recent deed or title to the property. Note the Book and Page number. Deeds usually are catalogued according to the Book in which they are registered. If your recent deed indicates, for instance, that it is "listed in Book D, Page 332," find that page in Book D and read the document. One of the final paragraphs will make reference to the previous owner and the Book and Page where the earlier deed was registered. Keep reading backwards until you have located all the earlier owners. Note their names and dates of ownership as well as the Books and Pages on which each deed was recorded in the official ledger. This, then, is the Chain of Title.

If you do not have access to the most recent deed, there are helpers. Deeds are indexed according to "Grantee" and "Grantor." The former is the receiver of the property, the latter is the person who deeded it over.

Some Notes of Caution: First, in many states a deed only conveys ownership of the land. A house may, or may not, be expressly included in the deed. Each deed should be read carefully to note when there is a seemingly unexplainable rise in price. This usually means the erection of a building on undeveloped land. However, unless you can date the house to the same period, do not assume it is the same structure. A later house may have replaced the original.

Second, as you read each deed be sure you are tracing the same piece of property included in your nomination. In the early centuries most land holdings were large. Later, lots were broken into smaller parcels for individual homesteads and it is easy to lose track of a particular property. Therefore, every time new ownership is recorded, check the boundaries carefully. You want to be sure you are following the same piece of property as it is subdivided.

I find it very helpful to obtain an early map of the property, then photocopy it in a convenient size and carry it with me on my deed search. The map helps me envision boundaries, a task made more difficult when a deed uses archaic measurements such as "rods," "chains," and "links." Further, older maps often contain the names of neighboring landowners. Deeds often cite neighbors who share boundary lines with the property, so if the same names appear in similar locations on the deed and map, you can be sure you are on the right track.

The Surrogate's Office contains wills, probate records, inventories and appraisals of estates. Administrators or executors appointed to manage the inheritance of minors must file yearly returns and accounts. This material can yield information on land sales not recorded by deed because they passed through inheritance. You also may learn about family relationships, both good and bad, as well as property holdings, ownership changes and the wealth of the family involved. An alert researcher also is likely to pick up other intimate tidbits of family history!

Architectural Journals and Architectural and Construction Drawings are additional sources of data on building materials, including the dates and original appearance of buildings, alterations and architects. These often are found in the offices of municipal tax assessors, architectural associations or special libraries or collections such as The Athenaeum, 219 South 6th Street, Philadelphia, Pennsylvania. Founded in 1814, it houses an extensive collection of works on architectural and interior design. One of its major publications *The Biographical Dictionary of Philadelphia Architects, 1700-1930* by Sandra L. Tatman and Roger W. Moss is an important source of biographical information on Philadelphia area architects.

Building Permits found at local building inspectors' offices may contain the name of the architect, contractors, building plans, alterations, costs and building materials. Very early building construction did not usually require such authorizations. Later alterations, particularly those in the present century, did need such approvals.

Photograph and Post Card Collections at local historical societies as well as in libraries, universities and colleges often can provide information on original architectural or landscape features, especially when these may have been altered. Area antique shops and flea markets often yield such treasures. Also, don't overlook the possibility that such mementos may be found in family scrapbooks of your neighbors or previous owners of your house. A deed search will provide you with their names. Don't hesitate to interview anyone who may have information to offer.

Census and Church Records are uncovered easily. The former are located in state archives, local libraries and historical societies, the National Archives and its regional centers. The Federal Census that has been taken every ten years since 1790 to reapportion members of the House of Representatives contains information on population and has been microfilmed. The information uncovered can be important in making a case under Criterion B.

The earliest Federal Census available is 1790; the 1920 census is the most recent one released for public scrutiny. Usually these records are not made available to the public until 75 years after the census is taken in order to protect public privacy. The Federal Census did not list house addresses until 1880 and, although a regular 1890 census was destroyed by fire, some special schedules exist and can be found on three rolls of microfilm M407 in the National Archives.

Only population figures were gathered for the 1790 and 1800 censuses. For later years, the names and occupations of those who resided on the property during the census years and acreage, crops, livestock, ownership of the property, ethnic background, ages and literacy of the residents can be obtained. Check your library and local historical society for availability of census material.

A visit to parish and diocesan offices of religious denominations in your area can turn up birth, death, marriage, and baptismal records as well as other details.

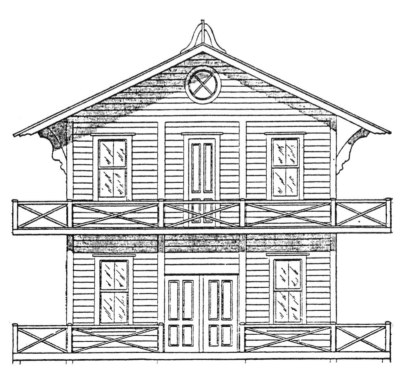

An office, formerly used as a boat clubhouse c. 1900

Local and Regional Branches of the National Archives have census data, Federal Survey Maps, thousands of Federal records on microfilm and, most important, guides to most of the collections in the National Archives. Regional centers are located in Boston, New York, Philadelphia, Atlanta, Chicago, Fort Worth, Denver, San Francisco, Laguna Niguel (California) and Kansas City (Missouri). For more information, contact the office of the National Archives and Records Administration, 7th Street and Pennsylvania Avenue, NW, Washington, DC 20408 or call 202-501-5402.

Genealogical Collections of Historical Societies, State and National Archives and Museums and Local Libraries can aid in associating your property with individuals and events. These records, often published privately as county, local and family histories, contain biographies of individuals, family anecdotes, even photographs of the people and their homes.

The Mormon Church (Church of Jesus Christ of Latter Day Saints) has a genealogical society and more than 200 family study centers throughout the country which may be used without charge. For information on the center closest to you write the Church's Genealogical Society, 50 East North Temple Street, Salt Lake City, Utah 84105.

Military Records and Pension Application Files yield varied information and are an important part of the National Archives. However, to use this material the researcher must know whether the subject was an officer or enlisted man and when and in what branch of the military he or she served.

Pension application files are a treasure trove of information on servicemen, their widows and children for the years 1775 to 1916. No Federal pensions were awarded to those who served in the Confederate Army during the Civil War. Until the Civil War these records are arranged alphabetically by veteran; later they are arranged numerically. Typical information on pension applications made by veterans, their widows or children include name, age, rank, military unit, period of service, birthplace and residence of the veteran, the widow's maiden name, marriage date and place, the names of children and their heirs, dates and place of their births, and date of their mother's death.

Also often found in pension application files are discharge papers, marriage, birth and death certificates, narratives of service events, details of battles and campaigns, letters, enlistment papers, etc. Most pension records are in the National Archives Records of the Veterans Administration.

Generally, these records contain information on volunteers in the military service, 1775-1902; Regular Army personnel, 1789-1912; Regular Army Officers, 1789-1917; Navy personnel, 1798-1885 and Navy officers, 1798-1902; Marine Corps enlisted men and officers 1789-1895; Coast Guard and earlier such organizations, 1791-1919. The military records include those who fought for the Confederacy, 1861-65. World War One draft records are part of the Selective Service System Record Group 163 in the Atlanta branch of the Federal Archives. For military records before World War One write to the National Archives, Washington, D.C. 20408.

The National Personnel Records Center (NPRC), St. Louis, Missouri, has information on military service after the above dates. Information can be obtained by making requests on form 180, "Request Pertaining to Military Records." Send the form to NPRC, 9700 Page Blvd., St. Louis, MO 63132. The form is available from the NPRC, local VA offices and the Government Printing Offices and Federal Information Centers.

The National Archives also contain service records of those who were volunteers in all campaigns from the American Revolution to the Philippines Insurrection and World War One draft records. The latter are found in the Atlanta Branch of the National Archives.

Records of Soldiers' Homes, 1866-1938, (referred to as Veterans Administration Homes after 1930) are valuable research aids. They are in Record Group 15 of the Records of the Veterans Administration, the National Archives. Record Group 231, Records of the US Soldiers' Home, the National Archives, also contain hospital and death records, but you must know the name of the home and date of admission or death.

Soldiers' Burial Records and Headstone Applications also may be helpful, although not every soldier who died in service is listed in the National Archives. There are records of burials in all national and military post cemeteries (Record Group 92, Records of the Quartermaster General) 1861-1914. From 1962 on, these burial records are in Record Group 410, Office of the Chief of Support Services.

Headstone applications usually were made by relatives of deceased veterans or veterans organizations or civic or government entities. The information in these records gives the name of veteran, military service, rank, place and date of burial, etc., and are arranged by state, county and cemetery. For those buried outside the United States, applications are alphabetical by country of burial and name of deceased.

Newspapers are a rich font of information. Most often available on microfilm at local libraries, historical societies and the library departments of newspapers, they contain business annoucements, advertisements, birth, marriage and death announcements. The latter provide the names of survivors, places of burial, dates of birth, military service, cause of death and women's maiden names. You may find a photograph of the deceased. Society and gossip columns are full of articles about local developers, the activities of builders and architects, description of houses, planned alterations and additions, social events and new neighbors, etc.

News clippings of the old *New York Sun* from the turn of the century through World War II, arranged by names and subjects, may be found in the Annex of the New York Public Library, 521 West 43rd Street, New York, NY 10036. The Annex also holds the newspapers from many states and foreign countries, including the *London Times*.

Cemeteries and Cemetery Records offer dates of birth and death, next of kin and cause of death. Often gravestones are the only remaining records of this data as well as place of birth, occupation, military service, medals and honors, parents' names, ethnicity, social status, etc. During the 1930s some state Works Progress Administration (WPA) projects included the inventorying of local cemeteries. Check your local/regional historical society for availability.

Military Bounty Land Warrants and Land Records give accounts of land promised as an inducement for military service and transactions relating to the granting of free land to individuals. These accounts also show private land claims arising from this country's acquisition of land from another country as when California was ceded by Mexico after the Mexican War. Private land claims are arranged by state or geographic area and public land claims are arranged by state.

Such land records may provide information as to when and where buildings were placed on homesteads, maps drawn to identify the claims, marital and family status of claimants and their national origins. Such material may prove a property's association with a person or event and aid in meeting Criterions A and B.

For bounty land warrant application files, see the Records of the Veterans Administration. For Land and Homestead records, see the Records of the Bureau of Land Management, Washington, DC 20240.

Immigrant and Passenger Arrival Lists also are available at the National Archives and branches under the heading of US Custom Service Records, most of which document arrivals for many Atlantic Ocean and Gulf of Mexico ports, but only between 1820 and 1945. There are a few lists for 1920 arrivals at San Francisco and those are available only at that archive division.

Generally kept by ship captains, customs and immigration officials, earlier passenger arrival records are difficult to read because they were hand written and not all have been microfilmed. After 1882 records had to be maintained by federal immigration officials. Eventually, standardized forms were developed that contained the name of the ship, its captain, ports of arrival and departure and name, age, sex, marital status, occupation, nationality, last residence, final destination, etc. of passengers. Later, race and the name and address of the nearest relative in the native country were added.

Much as with its work on cemetery records, the WPA compiled alphabetical card indexes of passenger lists for the Immigration and Naturalization Service during the 1930s and they are on microfilm. Such lists exist for Baltimore, 1820-1897; Boston, 1848-1891; New York, 1820-1846, and Philadelphia, 1800-1906. The cards contain information on each passenger that includes name, age, sex, marital status, occupation, nationality, last permanent address, destination, port of entry, name of vessel and date of arrival. However, like the cemetery records, the indexes are incomplete and may contain errors. Make every effort to cross-reference the information.

It will be easier to find information about an individual in these immense records which contain hundreds of names for each year if you know the port, date of entry and ship name. This is especially true when searching the records of the ports of New York and Philadelphia.

Records of Native Americans and African Americans also are contained in the National Archives. Most of the Native American material concerns western tribes and is grouped in the records of the Bureau of Indian Affairs. Generally, all records of federal agencies may have information on Native Americans; sometimes tribes are specifically identified as such in the enlistment papers for Indian Scouts who served from 1866 to 1914.

Federal population censuses rarely identified individuals as American Indians except for a special 1880 census of Indians living near military installations in the states of Washington, the Dakotas and California.

Census lists for 1885-1940 submitted by each agent of the Bureau of Indian Affairs are on microfilm and arranged alphabetically by name of Indian Agency, then by tribe, then chronologically. To locate just one individual, a researcher must read through all entries for each tribe. However, after 1916, individual names were listed alphabetically.

Indian removal records list tribes that gave up their native lands to move further west. Enrollment records of the Eastern Cherokee also exist for individual tribal members who sought reimbursement for their land during the mid-19th and early 20th centuries.

Other information concerning Native Americans, available at the National Archives, Washington, DC, or one of its regional centers includes annuity payments made under treaty to certain tribal members; land allotment records; employee records, individual histories of students who attended Federal Indian Schools, Indian School Records; school reports, marriage registers, birth, death and sick and injured (Sanitary) records.

Records of African Americans also may be found in the National Archives although race is not always mentioned except in population censuses. Nonwhites were not listed by name in a Federal Census until 1870. Until then only freemen who were heads of households were listed by name; slaves were entered as statistics, i.e., the number held by each named owner, their color, sex and age.

Records of black Americans who served in American wars are contained in federal military records. Information on regiments of United States Colored Troops (USCT) are in the compiled military service records of the Civil War and arranged according to branch of service (Army, Navy, Marine Corps) and then alphabetically.

The Freedmen's Bureau, established by Congress following the Civil War, helped former slaves adapt to their new status. It helped them relocate, legalize common-law marriages, collect pensions, feed the destitute and perform other similar social services.

Records of the Washington, DC office of the Freedmen's Bureau contain marriage certificates, reports of marriages and proofs of marriages arranged by state in which the marriage was performed. Not all states are represented and it is important to know where the marriage was performed in order to locate a specific one. The collection may offer information on names and addresses of the parties and the person who performed the marriage, the ages and complexions of the bride and groom, the parents and the children by the present and any previous unions.

Another group of records, those of the various southern state field offices of the Freedmen's Bureau, contain similar information but mainly for Arkansas, Kentucky, Louisiana and Mississippi. Both groups of records are on microfilm.

Finally, other related Freedmen's Bureau records include accounts of slaves in the District of Columbia, emancipation or manumission papers, and records relating to the slave trade.

The National Archives and Its Regional Centers have several other miscellaneous collections including Records of the US District Courts; Pardon and Parole Records; Extradition Records; US Secret Service Records (mainly case files of counterfeiters); Records of the District of Columbia; Civilian Records from Army Posts; Records of Americans Abroad (including births, marriages and death notices); Passport Records; Naturalization Records; Tax Assessment Lists for the Civil War Period, and the Historical Records Survey, a project of the WPA as part of the New Deal which provided jobs for the unemployed. Also, look for Cartographic Records, such as census enumeration district maps, 1880-1960, and General Records, such as census enumeration district maps, 1880-1960 and General Land Office Records and Military Maps of the United States.

A simply executed two and a half story Colonial-style home. This late 18th century Georgian structure has an unadorned box cornice, symmetrical facade, six over six window panes in a double hung sash and gable roof. The Greek Revival pedimented portico is a later addition.

OTHER EXCELLENT GENEALOGICAL SOURCES ARE:

The New York Public Library
5th Avenue and 42nd Street
New York, NY 10018

Library of Congress
Local History and Reading Room
First Street and Independence Avenue
Washington, DC 20408

African-American Family
History Association
P.O. Box 115268
Atlanta, GA 30310

Dallas Public Library
1515 Young Street
Dallas, TX 75201

New England
Genealogical Society
101 Newbury Street
Boston, MA 02116

Allen County Public Library
301 West Wayne Street
Fort Wayne, IN 46802

Daughters of the American
Revolution Library
1776 D Street NW
Washington, DC 20006

National Genealogical Society
4527 17th Street N
Arlington, VA 22207

Jewish Genealogical Society
P.O. Box 6398
New York, NY 10128

Los Angeles Public Library
630 West 5th Street
Los Angeles, CA 90071

Western Reserve Historical Society
10825 East Boulevard
Cleveland, OH 44106

American Association for
State and Local History
1400 Eighth Avenue South
Nashville, TN 37203

Chapter Four

Completing the National Register Nomination Forms

The premise of this book is that the reader is interested in nominating a building, structure or object rather than archaeological sites or districts such as a lithic workshop or rock shelter of Eastern Delaware Native Americans, or the prehistoric village of an Anasazi tribe. Therefore, the specific guidelines that follow do not include instructions for describing archaeological properties.

The material in this chapter is based on information in the US. Department of Interior/National Park Service **National Register Bulletin 16-A** *which was prepared by Linda F. McClelland, Architectural Historian, of the National Register Branch, under the supervision of Carol D. Shull, Chief of Registration. Assistance was provided by James Charleton, History Division, Maureen P. Danaher, Historian, National Register Branch and Rebecca Shrimpton.*

Highland Township Library
205 W. Livingston, P.O. Box 277
Highland, Michigan 48357

Application

Form

NPS Form 10-900
(Oct. 1990)

OMB No. 10024-0018

United States Department of the Interior
National Park Service

National Register of Historic Places
Registration Form

This form is for use in nominating or requesting determinations for individual properties and districts. See instructions in *How to Complete the National Register of Historic Places Registration Form* (National Register Bulletin 16A). Complete each item by marking "x" in the appropriate box or by entering the information requested. If an item does not apply to the property being documented, enter "N/A" for "not applicable." For functions, architectural classification, materials, and areas of significance, enter only categories and subcategories from the instructions. Place additional entries and narrative items on continuation sheets (NPS Form 10-900a). Use a typewriter, word processor, or computer, to complete all items.

1. Name of Property

historic name _____

other names/site number _____

2. Location

street & number _____ ☐ not for publication

city or town _____ ☐ vicinity

state _____ code _____ county _____ code _____ zip code _____

3. State/Federal Agency Certification

As the designated authority under the National Historic Preservation Act, as amended, I hereby certify that this ☐ nomination ☐ request for determination of eligibility meets the documentation standards for registering properties in the National Register of Historic Places and meets the procedural and professional requirements set forth in 36 CFR Part 60. In my opinion, the property ☐ meets ☐ does not meet the National Register criteria. I recommend that this property be considered significant ☐ nationally ☐ statewide ☐ locally. (☐ See continuation sheet for additional comments.)

_____
Signature of certifying official/Title   Date

_____
State of Federal agency and bureau

In my opinion, the property ☐ meets ☐ does not meet the National Register criteria. (☐ See continuation sheet for additional comments.)

_____
Signature of certifying official/Title   Date

_____
State or Federal agency and bureau

4. National Park Service Certification

I hereby certify that the property is:

☐ entered in the National Register.
   ☐ See continuation sheet.
☐ determined eligible for the
   National Register
   ☐ See continuation sheet.
☐ determined not eligible for the
   National Register.
☐ removed from the National
   Register.
☐ other, (explain:) _____

Signature of the Keeper   Date of Action

_____

_____

_____

_____

_____

27

5. Classification

Ownership of Property
(Check as many boxes as apply)

☐ private
☐ public-local
☐ public-State
☐ public-Federal

Category of Property
(Check only one box)

☐ building(s)
☐ district
☐ site
☐ structure
☐ object

Number of Resources within Property
(Do not include previously listed resources in the count.)

Contributing   Noncontributing

_____ buildings

_____ sites

_____ structures

_____ objects

_____ Total

Name of related multiple property listing
(Enter "N/A" if property is not part of a multiple property listing.)

_____

Number of contributing resources previously listed in the National Register

_____

6. Function or Use

Historic Functions
(Enter categories from instructions)

_____
_____
_____
_____
_____
_____
_____
_____
_____

Current Functions
(Enter categories from instructions)

_____
_____
_____
_____
_____
_____
_____
_____
_____

7. Description

Architectural Classification
(Enter categories from instructions)

_____
_____
_____

Materials
(Enter categories from instructions)

foundation _____

walls _____

_____

roof _____

other _____

_____

Narrative Description
(Describe the historic and current condition of the property on one or more continuation sheets.)

8. Statement of Significance

Applicable National Register Criteria
(Mark "x" in one or more boxes for the criteria qualifying the property for National Register listing.)

☐ **A** Property is associated with events that have made a significant contribution to the broad patterns of our history.

☐ **B** Property is associated with the lives of persons significant in our past.

☐ **C** Property embodies the distinctive characteristics of a type, period, or method of construction or represents the work of a master, or possesses high artistic values, or represents a significant and distinguishable entity whose components lack individual distinction.

☐ **D** Property has yielded, or is likely to yield, information important in prehistory or history.

Criteria Considerations
(Mark "x" in all the boxes that apply.)

Property is:

☐ **A** owned by a religious institution or used for religious purposes.

☐ **B** removed from its original location.

☐ **C** a birthplace or grave.

☐ **D** a cemetery.

☐ **E** a reconstructed building, object, or structure.

☐ **F** a commemorative property.

☐ **G** less than 50 years of age or achieved significance within the past 50 years.

Areas of Significance
(Enter categories from instructions)

_____

_____

_____

_____

_____

_____

_____

_____

Period of Significance

_____

_____

Significant Dates

_____

_____

_____

Significant Person
(Complete if Criterion B is marked above)

_____

Cultural Affiliation

_____

_____

_____

Architect/Builder

_____

_____

Narrative Statement of Significance
(Explain the significance of the property on one or more continuation sheets.)

9. Major Bibliographical References

Bibilography
(Cite the books, articles, and other sources used in preparing this form on one or more continuation sheets.)

Previous documentation on file (NPS):

☐ preliminary determination of individual listing (36 CFR 67) has been requested
☐ previously listed in the National Register
☐ previously determined eligible by the National Register
☐ designated a National Historic Landmark
☐ recorded by Historic American Buildings Survey
  # _____
☐ recorded by Historic American Engineering Record # _____

Primary location of additional data:

☐ State Historic Preservation Office
☐ Other State agency
☐ Federal agency
☐ Local government
☐ University
☐ Other

Name of repository:

_____

29

10. Geographical Data

Acreage of Property _____

UTM References
(Place additional UTM references on a continuation sheet.)

1 [ ] [ ] [ ] [ ] [ ] [ ] [ ] [ ] [ ] [ ] [ ] [ ] [ ] [ ] [ ]
   Zone   Easting   Northing

2 [ ] [ ] [ ] [ ] [ ] [ ] [ ] [ ] [ ] [ ] [ ] [ ] [ ] [ ] [ ]

3 [ ] [ ] [ ] [ ] [ ] [ ] [ ] [ ] [ ] [ ] [ ] [ ] [ ] [ ] [ ]
   Zone   Easting   Northing

4 [ ] [ ] [ ] [ ] [ ] [ ] [ ] [ ] [ ] [ ] [ ] [ ] [ ] [ ] [ ]

☐ See continuation sheet

Verbal Boundary Description
(Describe the boundaries of the property on a continuation sheet.)

Boundary Justification
(Explain why the boundaries were selected on a continuation sheet.)

11. Form Prepared By

name/title _____

organization _____ date _____

street & number _____ telephone _____

city or town _____ state _____ zip code _____

Additional Documentation
Submit the following items with the completed form:

Continuation Sheets

Maps

A **USGS map** (7.5 or 15 minute series) indicating the property's location.

A **Sketch map** for historic districts and properties having large acreage or numerous resources.

Photographs

Representative **black and white photographs** of the property.

Additional items
(Check with the SHPO or FPO for any additional items)

Property Owner
(Complete this item at the request of SHPO or FPO.)

name _____

street & number _____ telephone _____

city or town _____ state _____ zip code _____

Paperwork Reduction Act Statement: This information is being collected for applications to the National Register of Historic Places to nominate properties for listing or determine eligibility for listing, to list properties, and to amend existing listings. Response to this request is required to obtain a benefit in accordance with the National Historic Preservation Act, as amended (16 U.S.C. 470 *et seq.*).

Estimated Burden Statement: Public reporting burden for this form is estimated to average 18.1 hours per response including time for reviewing instructions, gathering and maintaining data, and completing and reviewing the form. Direct comments regarding this burden estimate or any aspect of this form to the Chief, Administrative Services Division, National Park Service, P.O. Box 37127, Washington, DC 20013-7127; and the Office of Management and Budget, Paperwork Reductions Projects (1024-0018), Washington, DC 20503.

NPS Form 10-900-a
(8-86)

OMB Approval No. 1024-0018

United States Department of the Interior
National Park Service

National Register of Historic Places
Continuation Sheet

Section number _____ Page _____

1. Name of Property

historic name _____

other names/site number _____

(Use typewriter for forms. Computers or word processors can be used for narrative items and continuation forms)

GUIDELINES FOR ENTERING ANSWERS

For "Historic Name" use the name that most clearly indicates the property's historic importance, or the name in common use for the property during the time it achieved its significance. Use only one name here and limit it to 120 characters, including spaces and punctuation. Under Other Names / Site Number, list any additional historic names by which the property was known.

"Property" is the entire piece of land, acreage or real estate being nominated, whether a single building or several structures. A property may be named for a person or persons, events, characteristics, uses or historic associations such as *Mott, Peter House* (the original owner/builder of the house); or *Mott-Moore House* (first two owners of the house); or *Underground Railroad Station at Snow Hill* (significant use of the property).

Other ways of categorizing a house are by its address: *The House at Moore Avenue;* any unusual characteristic it may have: *The Old Frame House;* an accepted professional, scientific, technical or traditional name *Runaway Slave Haven.*

When a property is identified by the name of a person put the last name first, then first name and building type. If using the name of a well-known person, use the name as it is listed in the **Dictionary of American Biography**, i.e.: Paul, Alice Stokes not Paul, Alice.

If more than one person is involved in the property's significance, choose the most prominent or, if of equal importance, use as many names as are appropriate, *but* the entry should not exceed 120 characters. You may use the names of both husband and wife (*Mott, Peter and Elizabeth Ann House*) or just *Mott House.* I have used "The *Peter Mott House*" for several reasons: this is the name by which the structure is known locally and the name Peter Mott is well-known in the town.

If you are nominating a district, i.e. a significant contiguous group of sites, structures, buildings or objects historically or architecturally coupled, use traditional terms such as "*Snow Hill Village*" or generic terminology, "*Snow Hill Historic District.*" You may further define the district by using "*rural,*" "*residential,*" etc. as in *Snow Hill Village Residential District.*

If the property does not have an historic name enter " N/A;" enter the name or site number *you* think should be used followed by the word "preferred" and use the "preferred" name throughout the form. In Section 8 explain why you believe it is preferred. "Other Names" can be the name by which the property usually is called, or the name of the current owner, or its accepted use, i.e., *"Underground Railroad Station."*

If you are naming any property/site that does not have an historic or traditional name, leave the first line blank, or write N/A and under "other names/site number" use either the site number or its historical, traditional, cultural or geographic name such as*"Snow Hill Site."*

Borrowed from northern Italian villas and farmhouses, the Italianate-style wasequallyadaptable to urban and rural lifestyles; its non-conformity and boldness made itextremely popular in the mid 19th century. Note the fanciful brackets under overhanging eaves, low roof, cupola and longer, narrower windows. The "lie on your belly" windows, triangular pediments over the porch entry, second floor center window and cupola are elements of the earlier, Greek Revival style.

2. Location

street & number _____ ☐ not for publication

city or town _____ ☐ vicinity

state _____ code _____ county _____ code _____ zip code _____

GUIDELINES FOR ENTERING ANSWERS

Enter the address using house number, name of street (or road) where property is located (again, not to exceed 120 characters, including spaces and punctuation) *Example:* "121 Moore Avenue." Do not use Rural Postal Routes, such as RR or RFD. If the road is a highway route number and does not have a name enter that number and indicate whether it is a State, County or Town road. *For example:* "US 206," "SR 41," " County 541."

If the property does not have a specific address, give the names of the closest roads and describe where the property is located in relationship to those roads. *For example,* "2 miles east of the junction of US 206 and SR 38." You may use abbreviations to save space. If you are delineating a district enter either street and address numbers for the buildings and structures included, for example: "161-89 White Horse Pike and 17-39 and 16-42 Church Street" or give the boundaries "White Horse Pike (south side), Mouldy Road, Moore and Gloucester Avenues and parts of Warwick Road and Lawnside Avenues."

If you think the property needs protection from the public or there is a possibility of looting or vandalism, mark an X in the box "Not for Publication" and "Vicinity." The Park Service will withhold the address from public knowledge; the Federal Register will not publish the address, and give only the nearest city/town as location. If you wish to restrict the address mark X in "Vicinity" box and using a USGS map, enter the name of the nearest city/town in the "city/town" blank.
Enter the full name of the State or Territory where the property is located followed by the two-letter postal code. *Example:* New Jersey-NJ, Hawaii-HI, California-CA.

Enter the full name followed by the code number of the county, parish or equivalent where property is located. (See Appendix) Enter the postal zip code for the area where property is located. (Zip code books are available at your local post office)

3. STATE / FEDERAL AGENCY CERTIFICATION
The State and Federal Historic Preservation Offices will complete this section.

4. NATIONAL PARK CERTIFICATION
The National Park Service will complete this section.

5. Classification

Ownership of Property
(Check as many boxes as apply)

- ☐ private
- ☐ public-local
- ☐ public-State
- ☐ public-Federal

Category of Property
(Check only one box)

- ☐ building(s)
- ☐ district
- ☐ site
- ☐ structure
- ☐ object

Number of Resources within Property
(Do not include previously listed resources in the count.)

Contributing	Noncontributing	
_____	_____	buildings
_____	_____	sites
_____	_____	structures
_____	_____	objects
_____	_____	Total

Name of related multiple property listing
(Enter "N/A" if property is not part of a multiple property listing.)

_____

Number of contributing resources previously listed in the National Register

_____

GUIDELINES FOR ENTERING ANSWERS:

OWNERSHIP OF PROPERTY: Place an "X" in all boxes that apply.

1. Private property is property owned by an individual, group of people or organized body such as a church, corporation or native American tribe. In most cases an individual will nominate a property that is "private."
2. Public-local is government-owned property of a municipal or county government.
3. Public-state is government-owned property of a state government.
4. Public-federal is government-owned property of the federal government.

CATEGORY OF PROPERTY: Place an X in the box for the kind of property being described and nominated. Mark only one box. Use the official **National Register Property and Resource Types Chart** on the next page for Definitions and Examples.

35

NATIONAL REGISTER PROPERTY AND RESOURCE TYPES

TYPE	DEFINITION	EXAMPLES
BUILDING	A building such as a house, barn, church, hotel, or similar construction, is created principally to shelter any form of human activity. "Building" may also be used to refer to a historically and functionally related unit, such as a courthouse and jail or a house and barn.	houses, barns, stables, sheds, garages, courthouses, city halls, social halls, commercial buildings, libraries, factories, mills, train depots, stationary mobile homes, hotels, theaters, schools, stores, and churches.
SITE	A site is the location of a significant event, a prehistoric or historic occupation or activity, or a building or structure, whether standing ruined, or vanished, where the location itself possesses historic cultural or achaeological value regardless of the value of any existing structure.	habitation sites, funerary sites, rock shelters, village sites, hunting and fishing sites, ceremonial sites, petroglyphs, rock carvings, gardens, grounds, battlefields, ruins of historic buildings and structures , campsites, sites of treaty signings, trails, areas of land, shipwrecks, cemeteries, designed landscapes and natural features such as springs and rock formations, and land areas having cultural significance.
STRUCTURE	The term "structure" is used to distinguish from buildings those functional constructions made usually for purposes other than creating human shelter.	bridges, tunnels, gold dredges, firetowers, canals, turbines, dams, power plants, corncribs, silos, roadways, shot towers, windmills, grain elevators, kilns, mounds, cairns, palisade fortifications, earthworks, railroad grades, systems of roadways and paths, boats and ships, railroad locomotives and cars, telescopes, carousels, bandstands, gazebos, and aircraft.
OBJECT	The term "object" is used to distinguish from buildings and structures those constructions that are primarily artistic in nature or are relatively small in scale and simply constructed. Although it may be, by nature or design, movable, an object is associated with a specific setting or environment.	sculpture, monuments, boundary markers, statuary, and fountains.
DISTRICT	A district possesses a significant concentration, linkage or continuity of sites, buildings, structures, or objects united historically or aesthetically by plan or physical development.	college campuses, central business districts, residential areas, commercial areas; large forts; industrial complexes; civic centers; rural villages; canal systems; collections of habitation and limited activity sites, irrigation systems, large farms, ranches, estates, or plantations; transportation networks; and large landscaped parks.

CLASSIFYING A PROPERTY WHICH CONTAINS A SINGLE RESOURCE:
Under "Contributing" insert the number "1" alongside the type of property being nominated. Put the total at the bottom.

CLASSIFYING A PROPERTY CONTAINING MORE THAN ONE RESOURCE:
To classify a property which has a main resource and some related secondary sources, consider the main resource. For example, when nominating a house, garage, shed or barn, the property is a **building** because it is essentially used as a shelter; if the garage is attached to the house, the property is still a **building**.

A property is a **district** if there are a large number of contiguous sites, buildings, structures, etc., which historically are associated, or were planned to be used over a broad area such as a residential section or manufacturing complex.

If the property is a cemetery, it is classified as a site; if the cemetery also contains a gatehouse, the classification is still a site. If the nominated property is a bandstand or carousel located in a park, it is classified as a **structure**, because although it is functional, it was not created to provide shelter. If a subject is a statue or a monument, it is classified as an object because it is primarily artistic.

CALCULATING THE NUMBER OF RESOURCES WITHIN THE PROPERTY BEING NOMINATED:

Contributing Resource(s): A contributing resource (a building, structure, site or object) is one that *will add* to the historic associations, architectural qualities, or archaeological values for which a property is significant, either because it was on the property during the period the property attained significance, relates to that significance, has historic integrity or will yield important information about the period; or the contributing resource meets the National Register criteria independently. *For Example*, assume the property is the birthplace of a prominent person and also contains a rare hunting lodge designed by Frank Lloyd Wright; the lodge should be identified as a contributing resource and explained in Section 8: Statement of Significance.

Noncontributing Resource(s): A Noncontributing building, structure, site or object is one that does **not** add to those associations, qualities or values mentioned above because it *was not present* during the period of significance or does not relate to the documented importance of the property; or, no longer has historic integrity because it was altered or disturbed or is not capable of yielding information about the period; or does not meet the National Register criteria on its own.

COUNTING RESOURCES: Count only resources which are significant in size and scale; do not count trivial resources such as small sheds, grave markers, lean-tos, etc., unless they make an important contribution to the property's historic significance. *For example* , if the shed served as slave quarters on a plantation, include it.

Attached rowhouses should be counted as individual resources. Therefore, count 10 attached rowhouses as 10 contributing buildings.

Do not count covered walkways and promenades or additions separately, unless such attachments or additions were built as separate structures and later united with the main resource. Do not include gardens, parks, vacant lots or open spaces *unless* they contribute to the significance of the property. Then they should be listed as "sites."

Do not count fences, gardens, walkways, other landscape elements, etc. separately unless they are very important or large in size. An example would be a statue by a noted sculptor or a garden designed by a noted landscape architect.

Count a lighthouse with attached keeper's house as 1 contributing structure. A church with an adjoining historically associated cemetery may be listed either as one contributing site or 1 contributing building.

An important person's birthplace consisting of a residence, an icehouse and forge barn built during the residence's period of significance, 3 sheds, 2 garages and a packing house built after the period of significance will have 3 contributing buildings (the residence, icehouse and forge barn) and 3 noncontributing buildings (the 2 garages and packing house). The sheds are not counted.

NAME OF RELATED MULTIPLE PROPERTY LISTING: This nomination form should be used only for a single property. Therefore, enter N/A. A multiple property listing refers to a group of nominations that represent a type. *For example,* the nomination of several early motion picture houses found within one county might be typed as *Early Movie Theaters in Adams County, North Dakota.* Each movie theater would be listed on a separate registration form and, in addition, on a multiple property form.

NUMBER OF CONTRIBUTING RESOURCES PREVIOUSLY LISTED IN THE NATIONAL REGISTER: In most instances, "N/A" is the answer to be placed on this line.However, if you are nominating an historic district which contains 8 buildings already listed, write "8." If you are enlarging an historic district by adding 1 building to 23 buildings already listed, write "23."

6. Function or Use

Historic Functions	**Current Functions**
(Enter categories from instructions)	(Enter categories from instructions)

Use the official "**DATA CATEGORIES FOR FUNCTION AND USES**"
Chart on the next page for definitions and examples

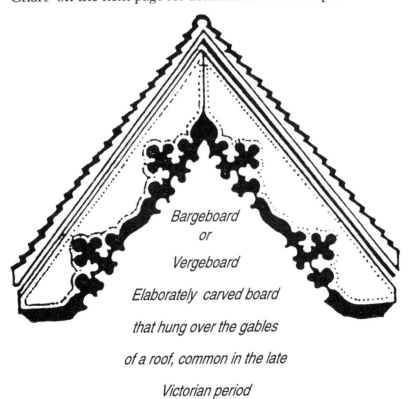

Bargeboard
or
Vergeboard
Elaborately carved board
that hung over the gables
of a roof, common in the late
Victorian period

DATA CATEGORIES FOR FUNCTIONS AND USES

CATEGORY	SUBCATEGORY	EXAMPLES
DOMESTIC	single dwelling	rowhouse, mansion, residence, rockshelter, homestead, cave
	multiple dwelling	duplex, apartment building, pueblo, rockshelter, cave
	secondary structure	dairy, smokehouse, storage pit, storage shed, kitchen, garage, other dependencies
	hotel	inn, hotel, motel, way station
	institutional housing	military quarters, staff housing poorhouse, orphanage
	camp	hunting campsite, fishing camp, summer camp, forestry camp, seasonal residence, temporary habitation site, tipi rings
	village site	pueblo group
COMMERCE /TRADE	business	office building
	professional	architect's studio, engineering office, law office
	organizational	trade union, labor union, professional association
	financial institution	savings and loan association, bank, stock exchange
	specialty store	auto showroom, bakery, clothing store, blacksmith shop, hardware store
	department store	general store, department store, marketplace, trading post
	restaurant	cafe, bar, roadhouse, tavern
	warehouse	warehouse, commercial storage
	trade (archeology)	cache, site with evidence of trade, storage pit
	trade (archeology)	cache, site with evidence of trade, storage pit

DATA CATEGORIES FOR FUNCTIONS AND USES

CATEGORY	SUBCATEGORY	EXAMPLES
SOCIAL	meeting hall	grange; union hall; Pioneer hall; hall of other fraternal, patriotic, or political organization
	clubhouse	facility of literary, social, or garden club
	civic	facility of volunteer or public service organizations such as the American Red Cross
GOVERNMENT	capitol	statehouse, assembly building
	city hall	city hall, town hall
	correctional facility	police station, jail, prison
	fire station	firehouse
	government office	municipal building
	diplomatic building	embassy, consulate
	custom house	custom house
	post office	post office
	public works	electric generating plant, sewer system
	courthouse	county courthouse, Federal courthouse
EDUCATION	school	schoolhouse, academy, secondary school, grammar school, trade or technical school
	college	university, college, junior college
	library	library
	research facility	laboratory, observatory, planetarium
	education-related	college dormitory, housing at boarding schools

DATA CATEGORIES FOR FUNCTIONS AND USES

CATEGORY	SUBCATEGORY	EXAMPLES
RELIGION	religious facility	church, temple, synagogue, cathedral, mission, temple, mound, sweathouse, kiva, dance court, shrine
	ceremonial site	astronomical observation post, intaglio, petroglyph site
	church school	religious academy or schools
	church-related residence	parsonage, convent, rectory
FUNERARY	cemetery	burying ground, burial site, cemetery, ossuary
	graves/burials	burial cache, burial mound, grave
	mortuary	mortuary site, funeral home, cremation area, crematorium
RECREATION AND CULTURE	theater	cinema, movie theater, playhouse
	auditorium	hall, auditorium
	museum	museum, art gallery, exhibition hall
	music facility	concert-hall, opera house, bandstand, dancehall
	sports facility	gymnasium, swimming pool, tennis court, playing field, stadium
	outdoor recreation	park, campground, picnic area, hiking trail
	fair	amusement park, county fairground
	monument/marker	commemorative marker, commemorative monument
	work of art	sculpture, carving, statue, mural, rock art

CATEGORY	SUBCATEGORY	EXAMPLES
AGRICULTURE/ SUBSISTENCE	processing	meatpacking plant, cannery, smokehouse, brewery, winery, food processing site, gathering site, tobacco barn
	storage	granary, silo, wine cellar, storage site, tobacco warehouse, cotton warehouse
	agricultural field	pasture, vineyard, orchard, wheatfield, crop marks, stone alignments, terrace, hedgerow
	animal facility	hunting & kill site, stockyard, barn, chicken coop, hunting corral, hunting run, apiary
	fishing facility or site	fish hatchery, fishing grounds
	horticultural facility	greenhouse, plant observatory, garden
	agricultural outbuilding	wellhouse, wagon shed, tool shed, barn
	irrigation facility	irrigation system, canals, stone alignments, headgates, check dams
INDUSTRY/ PROCESSING/ EXTRACTION	manufacturing facility	mill, factory, refinery, processing plant, pottery kiln
	extractive facility	coal mine, oil derrick, gold dredge, quarry, salt mine
	waterworks	reservoir, water tower, canal, dam
	energy facility	windmill, power plant, hydroelectric dam
	communications facility	telegraph cable station, printing plant, television station, telephone company facility, satellite tracking station
	processing site	shell processing site, toolmaking site, copper mining and processing site
	industrial storage	warehouse

DATA CATEGORIES FOR FUNCTIONS AND USES

CATEGORY	SUBCATEGORY	EXAMPLES
INDUSTRY/ PROCESSING/ EXTRACTION		
	industrial storage	warehouse
HEALTH CARE	hospital	veteran's medical center, mental hospital, private or public hospital, medical research facility
	clinic	dispensary, doctor's office
	sanitarium	nursing home, rest home, sanitarium
	medical business/office	pharmacy, medical supply store, doctor or dentist's office
	resort	baths, spas, resort facility
DEFENSE	arms storage	magazine, armory
	fortification	fortified military or naval post, earth fortified village, palisaded village, fortified knoll or mountain top, battery, bunker
	military facility	military post, supply depot, garrison fort, barrack, military camp
	battle site	battlefield
	coast guard facility	lighthouse, coast guard station, pier, dock, life-saving station
	naval facility	submarine, aircraft carrier, battleship, naval base
	air facility	aircraft, air base, missile launching site

DATA CATEGORIES FOR FUNCTIONS AND USES

CATEGORY	SUBCATEGORY	EXAMPLES
LANDSCAPE	parking lot	
	park	city park, State park, national park
	plaza	square, green, plaza, public common
	garden	
	forest	
	unoccupied land	meadow, swamp, desert
	underwater	underwater site
	natural feature	mountain, valley, promontory, tree, river, island, pond, lake
	street furniture/object	street light, fence, wall, shelter, gazebo, park bench
	conservation area	wildfire refuge, ecological habitat
TRANSPORTATION	rail-related	railroad, train depot, locomotive, streetcar line, railroad bridge
	air-related	aircraft, airplane hangar, airport, launching site
	water-related	lighthouse, navigational aid, canal, boat, ship, wharf, shipwreck
	road-related (vehicular)	parkway, highway, bridge, toll gate, parking garage
	pedestrian-related	boardwalk, walkway, trail
WORK IN PROGRESS	(use this category when work is in progress)	
UNKNOWN		
VACANT/NOT IN USE	(use this category when property is not being used)	
OTHER		

GUIDELINES FOR ENTERING FUNCTIONS

Using the chart above, select the category and subcategory that most accurately describe the property's primary **Historic** and **Current** functions. If a category has more than one name, choose the one that makes the best connection. *For example*, list a house as **"Domestic**/single dwelling;" list an amusement park as **"Recreation**/fair," a covered bridge as **"Transportation**/road related;" a grange as **Social**/meeting hall," a windmill as **"Industry/** energy facility."

Study the categories and subcategories carefully. Be specific. If there is no applicable subcategory, just enter the general category. If no category adequately describes the property's function, enter "Other" and use a term that makes a good fit for the function.

"Work in Progress" may be used if the property's use is changing. *For example*, The Peter Mott House once was used as a dwelling but is becoming a museum. If a property has many functions, select the leading or most important use.

If the nomination is for a district, select the function which *best describes the whole district*. *For example*, an artists' village which includes cabins, kilns, art gallery, etc.: **"Domestic/** village site," or for a resort hotel complex: **"Domestic**/hotel." Buildings *within* the district of exceptional importance also should be listed. *For example*, in the first illustration above, **"Museum/**art gallery" also should be listed under **"Domestic**/village site" if the gallery structure has architectural or historic significance of its own.

Select functions only for contributing resources which are present on the property and use only those which relate to the property's significance. These functions should be capable of documentation. Do not guess or speculate about possible uses. Select functions associated with the property, rather than with people or events that took place there. If the property served more than one function, multiple functions may be selected.

When selecting **Current Functions**, list the functions for both contributing and noncontributing resources.

7. Description

Architectural Classification
(Enter categories from instructions)

_____

_____

_____

Materials
(Enter categories from instructions)

foundation _____

walls _____

_____

roof _____

other _____

_____

Narrative Description (Describe the historic and current condition of the property on one or more continuation sheets.)

Use the official **Data Categories for Architectural Classification** on the next pages for definitions and examples..

TURRET:

A small tower

usually corbeled

from a corner

of a building and

projecting above it.

47

CATEGORIES FOR ARCHITECTURAL CLASSIFICATION

CATEGORY (GENERAL STYLE PERIODS)	SUBCATEGORY (SPECIFIC STYLE NAMES)	OTHER COMMONLY USED TERMS
NO STYLE		
COLONIAL	French Colonial	
	Spanish Colonial	Mexican Baroque
	Dutch Colonial	Flemish Colonial
	Postmedieval English	English Gothic, Elizabethan; Tudor; Jacobean or Jacobethan, New England Colonial; Southern Colonial
	Georgian	
EARLY REPUBLIC	Early Classical Revival	Jeffersonian Classicism; Roman Republican; Roman Revival; Roman Villa; Monumental Classicism; Regency
	Federal	Adams or Adamesque
MID-19th CENTURY		Early Romanesque Revival
	Greek Revival	
	Gothic Revival	Early Gothic Revival
	Italian Villa	
	Exotic Revival	Egyptian Revival; Moorish Revival
	Octagon Mode	

Categories for Architectural Classification

CATEGORY (GENERAL STYLE PERIODS)	SUBCATEGORY (SPECIFIC STYLE NAMES)	OTHER COMMONLY USED TERMS
LATE VICTORIAN		Victorian or High Victorian Eclectic
	Gothic	High Victorian Gothic; Second Gothic Revival
	Italianate	Victorian or High Victorian Italianate
	Second Empire	Mansard
	Queen Anne	Queen Anne Revival; Queen Anne-Eastlake
	Stick/Eastlake	Eastern Stick; High Victorian Eastlake
	Shingle Style	
	Romanesque	Romanesque Revival; Richardson Romanesque
	Renaissance	Renaissance Revival; Romano-Tuscan Mode; North Italian or Italian Renaissance; French Renaissance; Second Renaissance Revival
LATE 19th and 20th CENTURY REVIVAL	Beaux Arts	Beaux Arts Classicism
	Colonial Revival	Georgian Revival
	Classical Revival	Neo-Classical Revival
	Tudor Revival	Jacobean or Jacobethan Revival; Elizabethan Revival
	Late Gothic Revival	Collegiate Gothic
	Mission/Spanish Colonial Revival	Spanish Revival; Mediterranean Revival
	Italian Renaissance	
	French Renaissance	
	Pueblo	

49

CATEGORY (GENERAL STYLE PERIODS)	SUBCATEGORY (SPECIFIC STYLE NAMES)	OTHER COMMONLY USED TERMS
LATE 19TH AND EARLY 20TH CENTURY AMERICAN MOVEMENT	Prairie School Commercial Style Chicago Skyscraper Bungalow/Craftsman	Sullivanesque Western Stick; Bungaloid
MODERN MOVEMENT		New Formalism; Neo-Expressionism; Brutalism; California Style or Ranch Style; Post-Modern; Wrightian
	Moderne	Modernistic; Streamlined Moderne; Art Moderne
	International Style	Miesian
	Art Deco	
OTHER		
MIXED		More than three styles from different periods (for a building only)

GUIDELINES FOR ENTERING ARCHITECTURAL CLASSIFICATION, MATERIALS AND NARRATIVE DESCRIPTION

ARCHITECTURAL CLASSIFICATION: There are seven general architectural styles in America; each has one or more subcategories and identifying features which highlight the style. For help in identifying American architectural styles and terminology used to describe each style, see *American Architecture Since 1780: A Guide to Architectural Styles* by Marcus Whiffen. Also *Identifying American Architecture* by John Blumenson and *What Style Is It?* by John Poppeliers, et al.

The official chart on pages 48-50, used by the National Park Service, was adapted from the Marcus Whiffen guide. Use the chart to complete the item marked "Architectural Classification." Read down the left column (marked "Category") to select one of the prevalent styles of American architecture to which the nominated property belongs. Then choose one or more subcategories from the middle column. The subcategories denote a specific architectural style or stylistic influence on the property. If more than one subcategory is chosen, use a separate line for each and put the most important one first.

The right column offers other, frequently used, terms. If there are many entries, use a continuation sheet headed with the same name and number of the Section.

If none of the subcategories describes the architectural style/stylistic influence of the property, use only the category which relates to the time period of the property. On the next line enter "Other" and, using not more that 28 characters, enter an architectural term that will describe the style or stylistic influence. *For example:* **Late 19th & 20th Century Revivals. Other: Neo-Jacobean.** If you are unable to pinpoint a specific style/stylistic influence, just enter the category.

When nominating a property you can't describe by using any of the categories such as ships, bridges, certain folk or vernacular structures, enter "Other" with a descriptive term which uses no more than 28 characters. *For example*, Other: Naval Military Hangar. If the nominated property has no buildings or structures, enter "N/A."

If there are no categories or other listed terms that describe the building or structure being nominated, and there is no descriptive term that can be listed with "Other," enter "**No style.**" Employ an architectural guide to assist with terminology, using only a term which describes a design or construction type. **Don't confuse function with design.** Do not use the term "vernacular;" it is neither specific nor precise. The same applies to terms such as "workers' housing," "industrial building" "artisans' homes," etc.

DATA CATEGORIES FOR MATERIALS

EARTH

WOOD
Weatherboard
Shingle
Log
Plywood/Particle Board
Shake

BRICK

STONE
   Granite
   Sandstone (including Brownstone)
   Limestone
   Marble
   Slate

METAL
   Iron
   Copper
   Bronze
   Tin
   Aluminum
   Steel
   Lead
   Nickel
   Cast iron

STUCCO

TERRA COTTA

ASPHALT

ASBESTOS

CONCRETE

ADOBE

CERAMIC TILE

GLASS

CLOTH / CANVAS

SYNTHETICS
   Fiberglass
   Vinyl
   Rubber
   Plastic

OTHER

Materials: Using one or more terms from the above list, describe the primary exterior materials of the property; enter both historic and nonhistoric materials. Do not list hidden or interior materials. If the property has no buildings or structure enter N/A. Enter one category or subcategory in each blank for "foundation," "walls," and "roof." Under "Other" enter the principal materials of other parts of the exterior, such as chimneys, porches, lintels, cornices and decorative elements. Use a continuation sheet for additional entries, making sure to list them under the headings: "foundations," "walls," roof," or "other."

If the property is a building, complete the form for all the items listed and enter a category, or subcategory, if known, for each. If the property being nominated is an historic district, enter the major building materials visible in the district, listing the chief ones first.

If the property is a structure or object, complete: "foundation," "walls," "roof," only if they are present. *For example* : a covered bridge could have all three of these, but such features would not be present on a ship or truss bridge. In the latter case, use "Other" and qualify the exterior feature by entering "deck" for a ship; "triple span arch" for a bridge.

Narrative Description: In this section you are asked to describe the physical characteristics of the property. Use as many continuation sheets as you need. A typewriter or word processor should be used for narratives. Begin and end each sheet with a complete paragraph. Head each sheet with the Section and Page number; the name of the property, the municipality, county and state in which it is located.

Using your architectural guide, and in commonly used architectural terms, describe the complete setting, buildings and structures and all other resources on the property. Include any landscape features and major changes made to the property since its construction or period of significance. If the description includes regional or local terms not ordinarily used, explain them. *For example:* **"viga,"** found in Spanish Colonial and Pueblo architecture, is one of a series of wooden beams that project through the walls as support for the roof of a structure.

The opening paragraph should *summarize* the distinguishing aspects of the property and provide a word picture of its setting, size, architectural style, manner of construction, notable features, the condition of the property and whether its historic integrity is intact. Historic integrity would indicate whether it has been moved from another location and if its architecture, landscape design, building materials and general setting remain unchanged from its original period.

Having gathered all the necessary information about the property, it is extremely important to present it in a well-thought out and logical sequence, using clear, simple sentences. In the following paragraphs provide additional information about the property, giving, if known, the names of the architect and builder, dates and precise details wherever possible. The presentation should be concise, well organized and consistent with the information already provided in Sections 5 and 6 and Section 7: Materials.

It is best to begin with a description of the exterior from the roof down, or the foundation up; from facade to facade and then go on to the interior, beginning with the basement, the first floor, proceeding to the upper floors, and then the attic. If the building or structure has undergone any alterations or additions it is important to include a thorough description of such changes and how they have affected the property.

In describing a property that has been restored or altered, *first outline the current appearance of a feature and then its original appearance and the changes*, noting the dates of occurrence, how much of the original material remains, the historical basis for the work and the effect of the work on the property's historic character. Also include the following information:

> 1. **The kind of building** or structure being described, i.e., dwelling, church, theater, gasoline station.
>
> 2. **The setting of the property,** i.e., a college campus, the center of an industrial park, or in a residential area.
>
> 3. **Specific features and decorative elements of the structure** such as porches, porticos, verandahs, attached sheds or lean-tos, windows and doors, chimneys, dormers, ornamentation such as quoins, dentils, columns, pilasters, brackets, mosaics, vergeboards, etc.
>
> 4. **The general characteristics of the property. Include:**
>   a. the number of stories and bays (door and window units; if a dwelling has 4 windows and 1 door on the first floor and 5 windows on the second floor, it is said to have "5 bays")
>
>   b. overall plan of the house such as "rectangular, center hall colonial" or "L-shaped side hall Federal style," etc.
>
>   c. construction materials and method of construction, i.e., "red brick laid in common bond" or a "fieldstone rubble foundation," etc
>
>   d. the shape of the roof, i.e., " hip roof," "gabled," etc.
>
>   e. if known, how structure was constructed, i.e., "post and beam," "balloon frame," etc.

5. Notable Interior Features such as stairways, paneling, chimney surrounds, floors, purpose of rooms (ballroom, reception room, butler's pantry), moldings etc.

6. Number, type and location of any outbuildings with dates, if known.

7. Elements such as roadways, landscaping, parking lots, etc.

8. Any deterioration or degeneration from neglect, vandalism, weathering, etc., and the effect this has had on the historic integrity of the property.

9. If the property has been moved from its original site, provide the date of the move, describe the setting, location and placement of the property both originally and after the move. Tell the reason for the move, how it was moved, and the effect the move and new location have had on the historic character of the property.

10. If landscape or open space adds significance to the property, the natural features should be briefly described with an indication of its historic appearance. Also include information on any landscape features such as vegetation, gardens, paths, walks, orchards, bodies of water, rock formations, land use which distinguished the property during its period of significance. *For example:* " A 300 year-old Japanese dwarf maple tree still stands on each side of the east entrance, as does the original walled kitchen herb garden. However, the majestic hemlock from which the estate derived its name was destroyed by lightning in 1976."

11. When nominating an industrial property where equipment remains, provide the type, date and function of the equipment or machinery and the relationship of the machinery to the historic operation of the property.

12. When nominating a group of buildings or a district, first describe the general character of the whole and then describe each building separately. If it is a large district, describe only the principal buildings and the common types of buildings, giving their condition, original appearance and any major changes made to them. Do this in a logical sequence, moving from building to building down each street in succession.

8. Statement of Significance

Applicable National Register Criteria
(Mark "x" in one or more boxes for the criteria qualifying the property for National Register listing.)

☐ **A** Property is associated with events that have made a significant contribution to the broad patterns of our history.

☐ **B** Property is associated with the lives of persons significant in our past.

☐ **C** Property embodies the distinctive characteristics of a type, period, or method of construction or represents the work of a master, or possesses high artistic values, or represents a significant and distinguishable entity whose components lack individual distinction.

☐ **D** Property has yielded, or is likely to yield, information important in prehistory or history.

Criteria Considerations
(Mark "x" in all the boxes that apply.)

Property is:

☐ **A** owned by a religious institution or used for religious purposes.

☐ **B** removed from its original location.

☐ **C** a birthplace or grave.

☐ **D** a cemetery.

☐ **E** a reconstructed building, object, or structure.

☐ **F** a commemorative property.

☐ **G** less than 50 years of age or achieved significance within the past 50 years.

Narrative Statement of Significance
(Explain the significance of the property on one or more continuation sheets.)

Areas of Significance
(Enter categories from instructions)

_____

_____

_____

_____

_____

_____

_____

Period of Significance

_____

_____

_____

Significant Dates

_____

_____

_____

Significant Person
(Complete if Criterion B is marked above)

_____

Cultural Affiliation

_____

_____

Architect/Builder

_____

_____

DATA CATEGORIES FOR AREAS OF SIGNIFICANCE

CATEGORY	SUBCATEGORY	DEFINITION
AGRICULTURAL		The process and technology of cultivating soil, producing crops, and raising livestock and plants.
ARCHITECTURE		The practical art of designing and constructing buildings and structures to serve human needs
ARCHAEOLOGY		The study of prehistoric and historic cultures through excavation and the analysis of physical remains.
	PREHISTORIC	Archaeological study of aboriginal cultures before the advent of written records.
	HISTORIC - ABORIGINAL	Archaeological study of aboriginal cultures after the advent of written records.
	HISTORIC - NON-ABORIGINAL	Archaeological study of non-aboriginal cultures after the advent of written records.
ART		The creation of painting, printmaking, photography, sculpture, and decorative arts.
COMMERCE		The business of trading goods, services, and commodities.
COMMUNICATIONS		The technology and process of transmitting information.

DATA CATEGORIES FOR AREAS OF SIGNIFICANCE

CATEGORY	SUBCATEGORY	DEFINITION
COMMUNITY PLANNING AND DEVELOPMENT		The design or development of of the physical structure of communities.
CONSERVATION		The preservation, maintenance, and management of natural or manmade resources.
ECONOMICS		The study of the production, distribution, and consumption of wealth, the management of monetary and other assets.
EDUCATION		The process of conveying or acquiring knowledge or skills through systematic instruction, training or study.
ENGINEERING		The practical application of scientific principles to design, construct, and operate equipment, machinery, and structures to serve human needs.
ENTERTAINMENT/ RECREATION		The development and practice of leisure activities for refreshment, diversion, amusement, or sport.
ETHNIC HERITAGE		The history of persons having a common ethnic or racial identity.
	ASIAN	The history of persons having origins in the Far East, Southeast Asia, or the Indian subcontinent.
	BLACK	The history of persons having origins in any of the black racial groups of Africa.

DATA CATEGORIES FOR AREAS OF SIGNIFICANCE

CATEGORY	SUBCATEGORY	DEFINITION
	EUROPEAN	The history of persons having origins in Europe.
	HISPANIC	The history of persons having origins in the Spanish-speaking areas of the Caribbean, Mexico, Central America, and South America.
	NATIVE AMERICAN	The history of persons having origins in any of the original peoples of North America, including American Indian and American Eskimo cultural groups.
	PACIFIC ISLANDER	The history of persons having origins in the Pacific Islands, including Polynesia, Micronesia and Melanesia.
	OTHER	The history of persons having origins in other parts of the world such as the Middle East or NorthAfrica.
EXPLORATION / SETTLEMENT		The investigation of unknown or little known regions; the establishment and earliest development of new settlements or communities.
HEALTH / MEDICINE		The care of the sick, disabled, and handicapped; the promotion of health and hygiene
INDUSTRY		The technology and process of managing materials, labor, and equipment to produce goods and services.

DATA CATEGORIES FOR AREAS OF SIGNIFICANCE

CATEGORY	SUBCATEGORY	DEFINITION
INVENTION		The art of originating by experiment or ingenuity an object, system, or concept of practical value.
LANDSCAPE ARCHITECTURE		The practical art of designing or arranging the land for human use and enjoyment.
LAW		The interpretation and enforcement of society's legal code.
LITERATURE		The creation of prose and poetry.
MARITIME HISTORY		The history of the exploration, fishing, navigation, and use of inland, coastal, and deep sea waters.
MILITARY		The system of defending the territory and sovereignty of a people.
PERFORMING ARTS		The creation of drama, dance, and music.
PHILOSOPHY		The theoretical study of thought, knowledge, and the nature of the universe.
POLITICS / GOVERNMENT		The enactment and administration of laws by which a nation, state, or other political jurisdiction is governed; activities related to political process.

60

DATA CATEGORIES FOR AREAS OF SIGNIFICANCE

CATEGORY	SUBCATEGORY	DEFINITION
RELIGION		The organized system of beliefs, practices, and traditions regarding mankind's relationship to perceived supernatural forces.
SCIENCE		The systematic study of natural law and phenomena.
SOCIAL HISTORY		The history of efforts to promote the welfare of society; the history of society and the lifeways of its social groups.
TRANSPORTATION		The process and technology of conveying passengers. or materials
OTHER		Any area not covered by the above categories

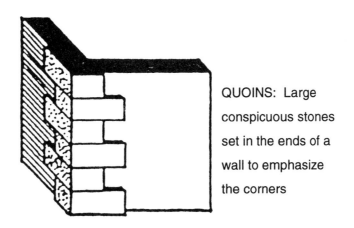

QUOINS: Large conspicuous stones set in the ends of a wall to emphasize the corners

GUIDELINES FOR ENTERING ANSWERS

Applicable National Register Criteria: The National Register Criteria are explained in Chapter One, Page 3. Mark "X" in one or more boxes to identify the criteria or standards that qualify the property for listing.

For nomination of historic districts which contain one or more properties that meet any of the individual criteria, mark "X" in the boxes that identify the criteria for which the property (or properties) are significant as well as for the district as a whole. *For example*, An historic residence known as "The Montebank House" has significance due to its early 18th Century French Colonial architectural style and it was also the home of an important early architect. Therefore the property is significant under both National Register Criteria B and C.

You may choose more than one area of significance in which the property qualifies for listing in the National Register. Also select one or more subcategories where possible. If selecting more than one category use a separate line for each with the most important first.

It is best to use the categories offered, However, is you cannot find a category that applies, enter "Other" and name the areas of significance. You *must* enter an area of significance for each Criterion checked on the form. Be sure that the area of significance you choose is supported by what you write in the **Narrative Statement.**

Criteria Considerations: Other criteria considerations are explained in Chapter One, Page 4. They provide special situations that allow for nomination of certain properties usually excluded from the National Register. If no special considerations apply, leave this section blank. If one or more special considerations apply, mark all that do apply. For an historic district nomination mark only those criteria that apply to the district as a whole, or to a major resource, or group, within the district.

Selecting Areas of Significance: If a property is significant under Criterion A, choose the category which relates to the historic event or role for which the property is significant. *For example*, the Peter Mott House is significant under Criterion A because of the Ethnic Heritage connected with it. The subcategory is "Black Social History," further defining indicates its association with the Underground Railroad.

If a property is significant under Criterion B, choose the category in which the significant individual either made, or was known for, his or her contributions. *For example*, the Peter Mott House also is significant under Criterion B because Mott was an important early African American pioneer in the pre-Civil War settlement.

If a property is significant under Criterion C, choose "Architecture" or other similar category which applies. The category chosen will depend upon the property and its importance. *For example*, the Peter Mott House also is significant under Criterion C because the house is representative of early settlers in the village. A church designed by Frank Lloyd Wright with stained glass windows by Louis Comfort Tiffany could meet Criterion B under "Architecture" and Criterion C under "Art."

Criterion D usually is for prehistoric properties under the category "Archaeology."

Do not confuse this section with the information on historic function requested in Section 6. "Area of Significance" refers to the field in which the property contributes to America's history, architecture, engineering, culture or archaeology. *For example*, the function of a museum is **recreation and culture,** and the area of significance is **entertainment/ recreation.** The function of a meeting hall is **social,** and the area of significance is **social history.**

Period of Significance: This refers to the interval of time during which a property began its connection with the people, events, activities, etc., or acquired the attributes which make it eligible for the National Register.

Select only the date(s) for the time span when the property achieved its significance. This may be one or more years or for several periods of time. Several time periods should be combined for one extended period. Continued use does not automatically support continuing the period of significance. *For example,* a structure may be significant for a pioneer homesteader who occupied it 1720-1790 and also have significance because it was occupied by a prominent legislator, 1820-1870. After 1870, a succession of summer visitors inhabited the house until it was left empty in 1990. The period of significance should be given as 1720-1880, *not* 1720-1990.

The property should continue to have its historic character or integrity intact for all the Periods of Significance selected. A property must be at least 50 years old to qualify for nomination, therefore, the significance must have taken place at least 50 years before the date of nomination.

If Criterion A has been selected, the Period of Significance is the date when the event took place. For Criterion B, it is the duration of time the property was associated with the person. For Criterion C, it is the date of construction and/or periods of any significant changes.

Significant Dates: This is the year(s) when the *major events(s)* took place which directly contributed to the property's significance. For example, where the property is significant because of its architect or designer, use the date of construction. If the importance of a property comes from the residency of a significant person, select those years. If the date marks the end of the operation of a community windmill and resulted in the migration of village inhabitants, select that date. If there are no specific dates within a broad Period of Significance enter N/A.

For example, suppose Criterion C has been selected with a Period of Significance encompassing the interval of the property's years of construction (1845-1865) and a major architectural alteration was designed by Henry Hobson Richardson in 1865. Enter "1865" as a significant date.

Significant Person: This should be completed only if Criterion B has been selected. Enter the full name of the person and *do not* use more than 26 characters including spaces and punctuation. Put the last name first, making it as complete as possible. If the person is listed in the *Dictionary of American Biography*, enter the name as it appears there. If Criterion B has not been selected, enter "N/A." If more than one important person is associated with the property, use the most important one on the form and list the others, in the order of their importance, on a continuation sheet.

Do not use the name of a family, fraternal/civic association or any other organization. You may use the names of one or more family members *only if* each of those persons contributed to the significance of the property under Criterion B.

Do not use the name of a property's architect or builder *unless* the property is significant under Criterion B for being associated with the life of that person as his/her home, studio or office.

Cultural Affiliation: This refers to the ethnographic culture to which a collection of artifacts or resources belongs. *For example*, "Navajo," "Sea Islander," "Shaker," "Italian-American," "African-American," "Ramapo." etc.

Architect / Builder: If you know the name of the person who designed, built, or engineered the property, enter his/her full name with last name first and do not use more than 36 characters, including spaces and punctuation. If the person is listed in the *Dictionary of American Biography*, enter the name as it appears there. Include any known craftsmen, landscape architects, artisans and artists, entering one name per line, using a continuation sheet, if necessary. If there is more than one architect, builder, etc., list the most important one first. If the architect or builder is not known, enter "unknown." If there is no building or structure on the property write "N/A." For a historic district, enter the known architects in the order of their importance to the district.

Use the names of architectural/engineering firms *only* if you do not know the name of the specific person involved. If the property's design comes from the standard plans of an agency or firm, enter the name of the firm. An example might be "Sears Catalog" or the "US. Corps of Engineers."

Guidelines for the Narrative Statement of Significance: In this section, using continuation sheets that are typed or word-processed, explain clearly and concisely *how* the property meets the National Register criteria listed in Chapter One. Begin and end each continuation sheet with a complete paragraph. Head each sheet with a Section and Page number, the name of the historic property and the municipality, county and state in which it is located.

Before developing your statement of significance, refer to the facts you have uncovered in Chapter Two, "Questions to be Answered." Include only those facts that frame and support the case for the property's historic significance and integrity. The Statement of Significance should confirm all the information you have entered in Section 8.

The first paragraph must summarize the property's significance. Specify the associations/ characteristics through which the property acquired its significance. That is, relate the historic events, activities, persons, architecture, aesthetic qualities, etc. that represent the historic framework for which the property is important to the community, state or nation.

Be specific as to how the property meets the National Register Criteria under which it qualifies and how it has contributed to each area of significance marked on the form. Relate the role of the important individuals or cultural affiliations marked on the form. Provide information on how the property meets the special standards for any criteria considerations marked on the form. *For example:*

> The Peter Mott House is a rare surviving example of a housing type associated with the early development of Lawnside, the only ante-bellum African-American community to later become an incorporated municipality in the State of New Jersey. It was the residence of Peter Mott, a free black farmer who served as minister at Snow Hill Church and founded its Sunday School in 1847, becoming the first superintendent of the second oldest African-American Sunday School in the area, organized c. 1792.

> It was here, according to impressive circumstantial evidence and oral testimony, that Mott lived and provided sanctuary to runaway slaves. The Peter Mott House meets the National Register Criterion A for a property associated with the Underground Railroad; Criterion B for its association with Mott, an important early settler in Snow Hill, and Criterion C as a rare example of an ante-bellum black landowner's home in Snow Hill.

Ensuing paragraphs should support the summary by presenting the history of the property and providing facts to explain how it meets the National Register criteria selected and any historic trends, frameworks, themes or patterns of development that relate to the property. *For example:*

> The Peter Mott House is associated with the history of resistance, individualism and achievement by blacks and whites in the abolition movment. Lawnside, an early 19th Century African-American community, was first known as 'Snow Hill' and appeared in maps as early as c. 1847. In 1840 Ralph Smith, a white Philadelphia abolitionist, gaveto the residents land he owned along Warwick Road between the present day boroughs of Barrington and Haddonfield, and designed a formal village which he named 'Free Haven' to signify its role as a refuge from slavery. The lots were sold at low prices to provide homesites for free blacks.

Give a brief chronological history of the property and select, and briefly discuss, those facts about the property that support your reasons for stating its importance. Do this for each area of significance selected and show its connection to each of the National Register criteria marked in Section 8. Be specific in all references giving dates, proper names, etc. *For example:*

> Miss Doris Scott, now in her late 70s, recalled her grandmother telling her that Peter Mott used to take slaves in his wagon to Quakers in Haddonfield. Miss Scott's grandmother, Mary Williams Bell (1850-1938), may have been passing on information told by her parents. Deeds and maps in the possession of Miss Scott show that the Bell home bordered the Mott property; the Bell family attended Mott's church. Mary Williams Bell undoubtedly knew Mott.

9. Major Bibliographical References

Bibliography
(Cite the books, articles, and other sources used in preparing this form on one or more continuation sheets.)

Previous documentation on file (NPS):

☐ preliminary determination of individual listing (36 CFR 67) has been requested
☐ previously listed in the National Register
☐ previously determined eligible by the National Register
☐ designated a National Historic Landmark
☐ recorded by Historic American Buildings Survey
  # _____
☐ recorded by Historic American Engineering Record # _____

Primary location of additional data:

☐ State Historic Preservation Office
☐ Other State agency
☐ Federal agency
☐ Local government
☐ University
☐ Other
Name of repository:

_____

GUIDELINES FOR ENTERING ANSWERS

"Previous documentation on file" refers to earlier actions taken by the National Park Service in respect to the property being nominated. *For example*, if the property was recorded in the Historic American Building Survey (HABS), you should mark an "X" in this box and give the survey number. Mark an "X" in the appropriate box if a preliminary determination was made about the property.

If additional documentation is available about the property, mark an "X" in the proper box and enter the name of any such repository, excluding the State Historic Preservation Office (SHPO). *For example*, if the repository is the Historical Society of Fairfax County, Virginia, mark an "X" in the "Other" box and fill in that organization's name.

Use continuation sheets to enter the bibliographic material. Head each sheet with the Section and Page number, the name of the property and municipality, county and state in which it is located. Enter only the primary and secondary sources used to document the property such as diaries and journals, letters, inventories, wills and deeds, census material, newspaper and magazine articles, etc. Do not put in encyclopediae or other such general references, unless they contain specific information about the property. If you have used both manuscripts and published materials, list the items under two separate categories.

Use one of the standard bibliographical manuals such as E.B. White's A *Manual of Style* or K. Turabian's A *Manual for Writers*. Sources should be listed alphabetically, last name first. Underline the title of printed materials, give the publisher, place, and year or publication. This data usually is printed on the page of a publication which contains the copyright information. *For example:*
McGowan, James A. Stationmaster on the Underground Railroad.
  Pennsylvania: Whimsey Press, 1977.

When citing unpublished materials or manuscripts, tell where the materials are located. *For example,* "American Negro Historical Society Papers in the Leon Gardiner Collection, Historical Society of Pennsylvania." For magazine or periodical articles, list the name, volume number and date of the periodical. If your source is an interview, give the date of the interview, the name of the interviewer, name and title of person interviewed and where tape or transcript of the interview is stored. As an alternative, such information could be provided in the body of the narrative.

If there is no USGS map for the area, a State Highway map may be used. Follow the same directions given above for the USGS map.

A modest or low-style Greek Revival house. Simplicity is the hallmark of this ubiquitous style built, with regional variations, c. 1820-1840. Here one can see the transition to the Gothic Revival-style.

10. Geographical Data

Acreage of Property _____

UTM References
(Place additional UTM references on a continuation sheet.)

1 ☐☐ ☐☐☐☐☐☐ ☐☐☐☐☐☐☐
  Zone   Easting   Northing

2 ☐☐ ☐☐☐☐☐☐ ☐☐☐☐☐☐☐

3 ☐☐ ☐☐☐☐☐☐ ☐☐☐☐☐☐☐
  Zone   Easting   Northing

4 ☐☐ ☐☐☐☐☐☐ ☐☐☐☐☐☐☐
  ☐ See continuation sheet

Verbal Boundary Description
(Describe the boundaries of the property on a continuation sheet.)

Boundary Justification
(Explain why the boundaries were selected on a continuation sheet.)

GUIDELINES FOR ENTERING ANSWERS

In this section you are to give the number of acres that comprise the property. You define the boundaries of the property nominated, explain why you chose those boundaries and give the Universal Transverse Mercator (UTM) grid references for its location.

When entering the number of acres that make up the property, be accurate to the nearest whole acre, unless you know the exact number and fraction. If the property is under one acre, state "less than one acre." This information is usually found on Tax Assessors' maps.

A USGS map and a unique device known as a UTM counter are required to determineUTM References. Most State Historic Preservation offices will fill in this information for you.

Selecting Boundaries: Select only those boundaries which will fully include all the important historic resources such as buildings, additions, and land area of the property being nominated. Include areas that directly contribute to the significance of the property. Once the boundaries are selected, no areas can be excluded from listing in the National Register. Sections that are within the boundaries but are not significant or that lack integrity, should be listed as "noncontributing."

Be sure to select boundaries which will include all important historic sites, such as buildings, additions and land area of the property being nominated. Include areas where the historic events occurred. Remember, the area within must retain its historic integrity and be directly associated with the significant event. Leave out those sections which have not kept their character. *For example,* a 17th Century log cabin sits on a piece of land adjacent to a contemporary home for the caretaker. Choose boundaries which include only the log cabin.

If the property nominated is a sculpture or other object, the boundaries can be only that piece of land or water occupied by the structure. An example is *The Bennington (Vermont) Battlefield Monument.*

If nominating an architectural or historic district, boundaries selected should include only the area containing the important collection of buildings being designated. *For example,* if a group of Victorian period homes is broken by something like a modern service station, a strip shopping mall or contemporary residences, the boundaries used should exclude these intrusions. Although districts may contain disconnected components, what is included must relate to National Register criteria. The integrity of the buildings and their relative significance will help you describe the edges of boundaries.

In delineating boundaries, the best choices are either boundaries legally recorded on the deed; the Lot and Block number from a tax assessor's map, or a legal parcel number.

If recorded boundaries cannot be used, select any natural topographic features such as mountains, ridges, rivers, forests, etc. If there are no natural features, look for manmade definitions such as walls, fences, curbs, roads and streets, etc. For large properties, inspection of the USGS map will be helpful by indicating contour lines and topographic features which can be used.

The Verbal Boundary Description: A Verbal Boundary Description can be as simple as "Block 44, Lot 19, Borough of Lawnside, Camden County, New Jersey." To include only a portion of a legally recorded boundary, you may write "Southwest two-thirds of Lot 19" or "the northern half of Lot 19" or "the western 40 feet of Lot 19."

Other possible Verbal Boundary Descriptions:

• A tax map, plat, or local planning board map drawn to a minimum scale of 1" = 200' may be used. *For example,* on a continuation sheet under the "Verbal Boundary Description" write "The boundaries of the John Peter Zenger House are indicated on the accompanying municipal tax map of 1965." The scale, an arrow indicating north and the boundaries of the property as they relate to natural or manmade features must be clearly marked.

• A USGS map may be used if the property is very large and the boundaries correspond to section or contour lines on the map. Under "Verbal Boundary Description" write "The boundary lines are indicated on accompanying USGS map" and mark those boundaries on the map.

• If you have access to the property deed, and the area being nominated includes the entire property, you may use the boundaries described by the deed.

- You may describe the boundaries using street, geographic features, and property lines. List them systematically with dimensions. *For example*, "Beginning at the southwest corner of Locust Street, eastward 190' along the property line with 125 Locust Street to the southeast corner survey mark, then 600' north to the northeast corner of Locust Street, then190' west along the property line with 123 Locust Street to the northwest corner survey mark, then 600' south along the property lines with 7 South 18th Street to the point of origin."

- You may describe a small rural property of under one acre by providing the dimensions and single reference point. *For example*, "The property is a square parcel measuring 180' X 180' whose southwest corner begins 100' east of the smokehouse and southeast corner begins at the foundation of the icehouse."

- For an object or structure such as sculpture, a ship, bridge, etc., it is sufficient to give the location and extent of the property on which it is located. *For example*, "The monument has a diameter of 100' and is located at Monument Circle Park."

Boundary Justification: This explains why you have selected the boundaries given. *For Example*, "The boundary includes the entire parcel containing the Peter Moss House." How much justification you provide depends on the property. The example given is sufficient for the Peter Moss House because it is contained within the original lot. A larger property, or one with very irregular boundaries, will require more extensive justification. *For example*, "The boundary includes the farmhouse, outbuildings, orchards, walks, lanes and meadows that were originally part of Overbrook Farm and maintain their historical integrity. The portion of the original farm east of Kings Highway is not included because it has been subdivided into contemporary residential lots.

---

11. Form Prepared By

name/title _____

organization _____ date _____

street & number _____ telephone _____

city or town _____ state _____ zip code _____

This section identifies the person who has prepared and submitted the form and any affiliation, if applicable. This provides the SHPO with the individual who may be contacted in the event any question may ariseor it additional information is necessary

71

DOCUMENTATION DOs and DON'Ts

- **Continuation Sheets:** Each sheet should be typewritten or word processed and have a Section and Page number at the top. Pages must be numbered in order from beginning to end. Do not renumber from Page One each time you begin a new section. In other words, if you have 12 continuation sheets from any section, the next page number you use will be #13.

- **Maps:** A complete and original, 7.5 or 15 minute series, United States Geological Survey Map, clearly locating the property, must be included with the form. Do not submit a copy of the map, or only a piece of the map. Do not use adhesive labels and do not write in ink on the map. *Using pencil only,* writing in the margin with an arrow indicating the location on the map, print the name of the property, the municipality, county and state in which it is located. You may draw lines (in pencil) to enclose all sides of the boundaries or, if the property is present on the USGS map, circle the dot that corresponds to it.

  If there is no USGS map for the area, a State Highway map may be used. Follow the same directions given above for the USGS map.

  A detailed sketch map also should be included if the property is an historic district or includes a large number of buildings, structures, etc.. The map can be hand drawn or you can use an insurance, plat, birds eye, or area highway map. If possible, use archival paper and, if large, fold it to 8 1/2" X 11." If the map is not on archival paper, fold it to the same size and place it in an archival folder for that size.

  You may use more than one map if several are needed to display all the required information. Be sure the maps are identical and that each contains the name of the property or district, the municipality, county and state where it is located. Show the boundaries of the property, principal landscape characteristic, substantial-sized buildings, structures, objects or those which are significant. Each should be labeled with a name, number or coded symbol and noted whether it is a Contributing or Noncontributing resource. Do not use color as part of your coding technique as it will not reproduce. Be sure to include the approximate scale of the map, a north arrow, street names and highway numbers.

- **Floorplans:** Include a hand-drawn floor plan, one page per floor, showing location of rooms, windows, doors, interior walls, significant features, such as an interior well, cooking hearth, secret room, etc. Again, each page should be labeled with name of structure, municipality, county and state.

- **Photographs:** Clear, vivid black and white photographs, preferably 8" X 10", with borders and unmounted, should accompany the nomination. The smallest acceptable size is 3 1/2" X 5". Photos should reflect an accurate representation of the property and its historic integrity, including any additions, alterations and significant details.

  I prefer to photograph a building from both front and rear, being careful to capture both the main facade and one side view in each snapshot. I use a 35mm camera, zooming in on the structure and important interior and exterior features.

  If the setting of the property is important to its significance, I also photograph its surroundings. Take as many photographs as you need to show the property, its condition, significance, resources, etc. Make two sets of each and send both with the nomination form. Retain a photocopy of each photograph and keep all the negatives for your files.

  When photographing historic districts, show only the major building types and styles, principal buildings, important elements that define the character of the district, and typical Noncontributing resources. Streetscapes and aerial views are the easiest way to represent large areas. Be sure to key photographs to the detailed sketch map.

  If possible, take along a second 35mm camera loaded with color slide film in order to capture an identical set of slides which you can use if you are invited to make a color slide presentation before your State Historic Review Board.

  Do not use adhesive labels on the photos as they can fall off or damage the photo. The best way to label photographs is to use a soft lead pencil and print on the back of each the name of the property, municipality, county and state where located and photograph number. Use a continuation sheet to list the rest of the required information including the name of the photographer, date photo was taken, description of view indicating the direction of camera (example: "view of south and west elevations, looking northeast"), the number of the photograph and where the original negatives will be kept.

On the continuation sheet insert "PHOTOS" under "Section Number" followed by the page number. Then list the name of the property, the municipality, county and state where it is located. Skip a few spaces, type or print the heading of "PHOTO-GRAPHS." Then "the following information is the same for all photographs:"

1. Name of property
2. Locality of property
3. Name of photographer (your name or another)
4. Date photographs were taken
5. Where negatives are stored (person's name and full address)

Then describe each view and give the photo number.

1. Photo number (*For example* 1 of 12) Description of the view and direction camera is facing.
2. "Photograph 2 of 12" Description as in #1.
3. Continue until all photos have been identified

The Gothic Revival-style, with its strong vertical feeling and steeply pitched cross gabled roof, was popular during the early Victorian period, c. 1830-1860. The genre evokes medieval Europe and the patterned wall shingles lend a picturesque sense of romance.

OPTIONAL

Chain of Title

For a particularly old structure, I highly recommend that a "Chain of Title" accompany the nomination. Again, use a Continuation Sheet headed by the name of the property and municipality, county and state where it is located. Then print or type "Chain of Title" across the top of the sheet. Enter the date, skip several lines, enter "Grantor", leave more spaces sufficient for a person's name, enter "Grantor", leave more spaces and enter "Book/Page"

Under all this enter where the Chain of Title was collected. *For example*, "Camden County, NJ Register of Deeds." Then list, beginning with the most recent, under each heading, the date of the transfer of title, to whom title was transferred (Grantee) and who transferred it (Grantor) and the identifying deed book and page number where transfer was recorded. The Chain of Title ends with the earliest transfer or purchase of land.

Because a deed search should be the first step in uncovering information about an old house, the ensuring Chain of Title is not an additional step. By submitting this proof of your research, you will be able to document what has been discovered.

New information often comes to light through a deed search. You may discover whether and how the property has increased or decreased in size, how much the value of the property may have increased with the erection of a house, who the various owners were, their occupations, marital status, land use, who the neighbors were, and whether the property was sold, seized, granted or inherited.

The blank form on the following page can be used as a guideline

Historic Maps

Additionally, you should also submit, if available, copies of historic maps or photographs that document the property in its earlier state. This is especially useful if there have been additions or alterations.

CHAIN OF TITLE

Date	Grantee	Grantor	Book/Page

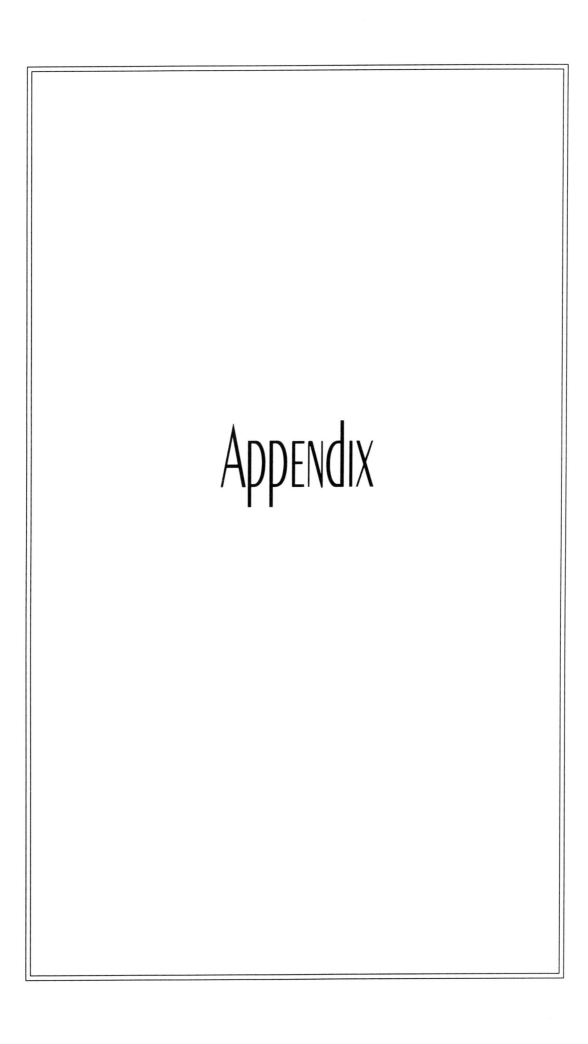

Appendix

The Federal-style buildings evolved in the period following the American Revolution. This New Jersey example is characterized by its two and one-half stories, gable roof, arched window dormers, front entry with transom and sidelights, paired-end chimneys, standing seam metal roofing and paneled shutters.

State Historic Preservation Offices

ALABAMA (AL)

State Historic Preservation Officer
Alabama Historical Commission
725 Monroe Street
Montgomery, Alabama 36130

ALASKA (AK)

Chief
History and Archaeology
Department of Natural Resources
Division of Parks and Outdoor
    Recreation
Anchorage, Alaska 99510-7001

AMERICAN SAMOA

Territorial Historic Preservation
    Officer
Department of Parks and Recreation
American Samoa Government
Pago Pago, American Samoa 96799

ARIZONA (AZ)

Chief
Office of Historic Preservation
Arizona State Parks
800 W. Washington, Suite 415
Phoenix, Arizona 85007

ARKANSAS (AR)

Director
Arkansas Historic Preservation
    Program
The Heritage Center, Suite 300
225 E. Markham
Little Rock, Arkansas 72201

CALIFORNIA (CA)

Office of Historic Preservation
Department of Parks and Recreation
P.O. Box 942896
Sacramento, California 94296-0001

COLORADO (CO)

President
Colorado Historical Society
Colorado History Museum
1300 Broadway
Denver, Colorado 80203-2137

CONNECTICUT

Director
Connecticut Historical Commission
59 South Prospect Street
Hartford, Connecticut 06106

DELAWARE (DE)

Director
Division of Historical and Cultural
Affairs
P.O. Box 1401
Dover, Delaware 19901

DISTRICT OF COLUMBIA (DC)

Deputy Mayor for Administration
1350 Pennsylvania Avenue NW
Room 507
Washington, D.C. 20004

FEDERATED STATES OF MICRONESIA (FM)

Historic Preservation Officer
Office of Administrative Services
Division of Archives and
Historic Preservation
FSM National Government
P.O. Box 490
Kolonia, Pohnpei 96941

FLORIDA (FL)

Director
Division of Historical Resources
Department of State
The Capitol
Tallahassee, Florida 32399-0250

GEORGIA (GA)

Commissioner
Division of Natural Resources
Historic Preservation Section
1252 Floyd Towers East
205 Butler Street, SE
Atlanta, Georgia 30334

GUAM (GU)

Director
Department of Parks and Recreation
490 Naval Hospital Road
Agana Heights, Guam 96910

HAWAII (HI)

State Historic Preservation Officer
Department of Land and Natural
    Resources
P.O. Box 621
Honolulu, Hawaii 96809

IDAHO (ID)

Director
Idaho Historical Society
210 Main Street
Boise, Idaho 83702

ILLINOIS (IL)

Director
Illinois Historic Preservation Agency
Springfield, Illinois 62701

INDIANA (IN)

Director Department of Natural Resources
608 State Office Building
Indianapolis, Indiana 46204

IOWA (IA)

Administrator
State Historical Society of Iowa
Capitol Complex
East 6th and Locust Street
Des Moines, Iowa 50319

KANSAS (KS)

Executive Director
Kansas State Historical Society
120 West 10th Street
Topeka, Kansas 66612

KENTUCKY (KY)

Director
Kentucky Heritage Council
Capitol Plaza Tower, 12th Floor
Frankfort, Kentucky 40601

LOUISIANA (LA)

Assistant Secretary
Office of Cultural Development
P.O. Box 44247
Baton Rouge, Louisiana 70804

MAINE (ME)

Director
Maine Historic Preservation
  Commission
55 Capitol Street
State House Station 65
Augusta, Maine 04333

REPUBLIC OF THE MARSHALL ISLANDS (MH)

Historic Preservation Officer
Secretary of Interior and Outer
Islands Affairs, Alele Museum
P.O. Box 629
Majuro, Marshall Islands 96960

MARYLAND (MD)

Executive Director
Historical and Cultural Programs
Department of Housing and
Community Development
45 Calvert Street
Annapolis, Maryland 21401

MASSACHUSETTS (MA)

Executive Director
Massachusetts Historical Commission
80 Boylston Street, Suite 310
Boston, Massachusetts 02116

MICHIGAN (MI)

Director
Bureau of History
Department of State
717 W. Ellegan
Lansing, Michigan 48918

MINNESOTA (MN)

Director
Minnesota Historical Society
690 Cedar Street
St. Paul, Minnesota 55101

MISSISSIPPI (MS)

Director
State of Mississippi Department of
  Archives and History
P.O. Box 571
Jackson, Mississippi 39205

MISSOURI (MO)

Director
State Department of Natural
  Resources
P.O. Box 176
Jefferson City, Missouri 65102

MONTANA (MT)

State Historic Preservation Officer
Montana Historical Society
225 North Roberts Street
Veterans Memorial Building
Helena, Montana 59620-9990

NEBRASKA (NE)

Director
The Nebraska State Historical Society
1500 R Street
P.O. Box 82554
Lincoln, Nebraska 68501

NEVADA (NV)

Director
Department of Conservation and
  Natural Resources
Nye Building, Room 213
201 So. Fall Street
Carson City, Nevada 89710

NEW HAMPSHIRE (NH)

Director
Division of Historical Resources
P.O. Box 2043
Concord, New Hampshire 03302-2043

NEW JERSEY (NJ)
State Historic Preservation Officer
CN-404
Trenton, New Jersey 08625-0404

NEW MEXICO (NM)

State Historic Preservation Officer
Historic Preservation Division
Office of Cultural Affairs
Villa Rivera, Room 101
228 E. Palace Avenue
Santa Fe, New Mexico 87503

NEW YORK (NY)

Commissioner
Office of Parks, Recreation and
    Historic Preservation
Agency Building #1
Empire State Plaza
Albany, New York 12238

NORTH CAROLINA (NC)

Director
Division of Archives and History
Department of Cultural Resources
109 East Jones Street
Raleigh, North Carolina 27611

NORTH DAKOTA (ND)

State Historic Preservation Officer
North Dakota Historical Society
ND Heritage Center
Bismark, North Dakota 58505

**COMMONWEALTH OF THE
NORTHERN MARIANA ISLANDS (MP)**

Historic Preservation Officer
Department of Community and
    Cultural Affairs
Commonwealth of the Northern
    Mariana Islands
Saipan, Mariana Islands 96950

OHIO (OH)
State Historic Preservation Officer
Historic Preservation Office
Ohio Historical Center
1985 Velma Avenue
Columbus, Ohio 43211

OKLAHOMA (OK)

Executive Director
Oklahoma Historical Society
Wiley Post Historical Building
2100 N. Lincoln
Oklahoma City, Oklahoma 73105

OREGON (OR)

State Parks Superintendent
525 Trade Street,SE
Salem, Oregon 97310

REPUBLIC OF PALAU (PW)

Historic Preservation Officer
Division of Cultural Affairs
Ministry of Social Services
P.O. Box 100, Government of Palau
Koror, Republic of Palau 96940

PENNSYLVANIA (PA)

State Historic Preservation Officer
Pennsylvania Historical and
  Museum Commission
P.O. Box 1026
Harrisburg, Pennsylvania 17108-1026

**COMMONWEALTH OF PUERTO
RICO (PR)**

State Historic Preservation Office
La Fortaleza
P.O. Box 82
San Juan, Puerto Rico 00901

RHODE ISLAND (RI)

State Historic Preservation Officer
Historical Preservation Commission
Old State House
150 Benefit Street
Providence, Rhode Island 02903

SOUTH CAROLINA (SC)
Department of Archives and History
P.O. Box 11669, Capitol Station
Columbia, South Carolina 29211

TENNESSEE (TN)

State Historic Preservation Officer
Department of Conservation
701 Broadway
Nashville, Tennessee 37219-5237

TEXAS (TX)

Executive Director
Texas State Historical Commission
P.O. Box 12276, Capitol Station
Austin, Texas 78711

UTAH (UT)

Director
Utah State Historical Society
300 Rio Grande
Salt Lake City, Utah 84101

VERMONT (VT)

Director
Division for Historic Preservation
58 East State Street
c/o Pavilion Office Building
Montpelier, Vermont 05602

VIRGIN ISLANDS (VI)

Commissioner
Department of Planning and Natural Resources
Nisky Center, Suite 231
No. 45A Estate Nisky
Charlotte Amalie, St. Thomas
Virgin Islands 00830

VIRGINIA (VA)

Director
Department of Historic Resources
221 Governor Street
Richmond, Virginia 23219

WASHINGTON (WA)

State Historic Preservation Officer
Office of Archaeology and Historic
Preservation
111 West 21st Avenue, KL-11
Olympia, Washington 98504

WEST VIRGINIA (WV)

Commissioner
Division of Culture and History
Capitol Complex
Charleston, West Virginia 2530

WISCONSIN (WI)

Director
Historic Preservation Division
State Historical Society
816 State Street
Madison, Wisconsin 53706

WYOMING (WY)

Director
Archives, Museums and Historical
Department
Barrett Building
2301 Central Avenue
Cheyenne, Wyoming 82002

Famous "Wedding Cake" House, Kennebunk, Maine was built in1826. TheGothic carpentry
work was added in the mid-Nineteenth Century

County Codes

ALASKA

010	Aleutian Islands
013	Aleutians East
020	Anchorage
050	Bethel
060	Bristol Bay
070	Dillingham
090	Fairbanks North Star
100	Haines
110	Juneau
122	Kenai Peninsula
130	Ketchikan Gateway
150	Kodiak Island
164	Lake and Peninsula
170	Matanuska-Susitna
180	Nome
185	North Slope
188	Northwest Artic
201	Prince of Wales-Outer K.
220	Sitka
231	Skagway-Yakutat-Angoon
240	Southeast Fairbanks
261	Valdez-Cordova
270	Wade Hampton
280	Wrangell-Peterburg
290	Yukon-Koyukuk

ALABAMA

001	Autauga
003	Baldwin
005	Barbour
007	Bibb
009	Blount
011	Bullock
013	Butler
015	Calhoun
017	Chambers
019	Cherokee
021	Chilton
023	Choctaw
025	Clarke
027	Clay
029	Cleburne
031	Coffee
033	Colbert
035	Conecuh
037	Coosa
039	Coington
041	Crenshaw
043	Cullman
045	Dale
047	Dallas
049	DeKalb
051	Elmore
053	Escambia
055	Etowah
057	Fayette
059	Franklin
061	Geneva
063	Greene
065	Hale
067	Henry
069	Houston
071	Jackson
073	Jefferson
075	Lamar
077	Lauderdale
079	Lawrence
081	Lee
083	Limestone
085	Lowndes
087	Macon
089	Madison
091	Marengo
093	Marion
095	Marshall
097	Mobile
099	Monroe
101	Montgomery
103	Morgan
105	Perry
107	Pickens
109	Pike
111	Randolph
113	Russell
115	St. Clair
117	Shalby
119	Sumter
121	Talladega
123	Tallapoosa
125	Tuscaloosa
127	Walker
129	Washington
131	Wilcox
133	Winston

AMERICAN SAMOA

001	Tutuila Island, Eastern
003	Tutuila Island, West
010	Eastern
020	Manu'a
030	Rose Island
040	Swains Island
050	Western

ARIZONA

001	Apache
003	Cochise
005	Coconino
007	Gita
009	Graham
011	Greenlee
012	La Paz
013	Maricopa
015	Mohave
017	Navajo
019	Pima
021	Pinal
023	Yavapai
027	Yuma

ARKANSAS

001	Arkansas
003	Ashley
005	Baxter
007	Benton
009	Boone
011	Bradley
013	Calhoun
015	Carroll
017	Chicot
019	Clark
021	Clay

023	Cleburne	119	Pulaski	059	Orange
025	Cleveland	121	Randolph	063	Plumas
027	Columbia	123	St. Francis	065	Riverside
029	Conway	125	Saline	067	Sacramento
031	Craighead	127	Scott	069	San Benito
033	Crawford	129	Searcy	071	San Bernardino
035	Crittenden	131	Sebastian	073	San Diego
037	Cross	133	Sevier	075	San Francisco
039	Dallas	135	Sharp	077	San Joaquin
041	Desha	137	Stone	079	San Luis Obispo
043	Drew	139	Union	081	San Mateo
045	Faulkner	141	Van Buren	083	Santa Barbara
047	Franklin	143	Washington	085	Santa Clara
049	Fulton	145	White	087	Santa Cruz
051	Garland	147	Woodruff	089	Shasta
053	Grant	149	Yell	091	Sierra
055	Greene			093	Siskiyou
057	Hempstead			095	Solano
059	Hot Spring			097	Sonoma
061	Howard	**CALIFORNIA**		099	Stanislaus
063	Independence			101	Sutter
065	Izard	001	Alameda	103	Tehama
067	Jackson	003	Alpine	105	Trinity
069	Jefferson	005	Amador	107	Tulare
071	Johnson	007	Butte	109	Tuolumne
073	Lafayette	009	Calaveras	111	Ventura
075	Lawrence	011	Calusa	113	Yolo
077	Lee	013	Contra Costa	115	Yuba
079	Lincoln	015	Del Norte		
081	Little River	017	El Dorado	**COLORADO**	
083	Logan	019	Fresno		
085	Lonoke	021	Glenn	001	Adams
087	Madison	023	Humboldt	003	Alamosa
089	Marion	025	Imperial	005	Arapahoe
091	Miller	027	Inyo	007	Archuleta
093	Mississippi	029	Kern	009	Baca
095	Monroe	031	Kings	011	Bent
097	Montgomery	033	Lake	013	Boulder
099	Nevada	035	Lassen	015	Chaffee
101	Newton	037	Los Angeles	017	Cheyenne
103	Ouachita	039	Madera	019	Clear Creek
105	Perry	041	Marin	021	Conejos
107	Phillips	043	Mariposa	023	Costilla
109	Pike	045	Mendocino	025	Crowley
111	Poinsett	047	Merced	027	Custer
113	Polk	049	Modoc	029	Delta
115	Pope	051	Mono	031	Denver
117	Prairie	053	Monterey	033	Dolores
		055	Napa	035	Douglas
		057	Nevada		

037	Eagle
039	Elbert
041	El Paso
043	Fremont
045	Garfield
047	Gilpin
049	Grand
051	Gunnison
053	Hinsdale
055	Huerfano
057	Jackson
059	Jefferson
061	Kiowa
063	Kit Carson
065	Lake
067	La Plata
069	Larimer
071	Las Animas
073	Lincoln
075	Logan
077	Mesa
079	Mineral
081	Moffat
083	Montezuma
085	Montrose
087	Morgan
089	Otero
091	Ouray
093	Park
095	Phillips
097	Pitkin
099	Prowers
101	Pueblo
103	Rio Blanco
105	Rio Grande
107	Routt
109	Saguache
111	San Juan
113	San Miguel
115	Sedgwick
117	Summit
119	Teller
121	Washington
123	Weld
125	Yuma

CONNECTICUT

001	Fairfield
003	Hartford
005	Litchfield
007	Middlesex
009	New Haven
011	New London
013	Tolland
015	Windham

DELAWARE

001	Kent
003	New Castle
005	Sussex

DISTRICT OF COLUMBIA

001	District of Columbia

FLORIDA

001	Aachua
003	Baker
005	Bay
007	Bradford
009	Brevard
011	Broward
013	Calhoun
015	Charlotte
017	Citrus
019	Clay
021	Collier
023	Columbia
025	Dade
027	De Soto
029	Dixie
031	Duval
033	Escambia
035	Flagler
037	Franklin
039	Gadsden
041	Gilchrist
043	Glades
045	Gulf
047	Hamilton
049	Hardee
051	Hendry
053	Hernando
055	Highlands
057	Hillsborough

059	Holmes
061	Indian River
063	Jackson
065	Jefferson
067	Lafayette
069	Lake
071	Lee
073	Leon
075	Levy
077	Liberty
079	Madison
081	Manatee
083	Marion
085	Martin
087	Monroe
089	Nassau
091	Okaloosa
093	Okeechobee
095	Orange
097	Osceola
099	Palm Beach
101	Pasco
103	Pinellas
105	Polk
107	Putnam
109	St. John
111	St. Lucie
113	Santa Rosa
115	Sarasota
117	Seminole
119	Sumter
121	Suwannee
123	Taylor
125	Union
127	Volusia
129	Wakulla
131	Walton
133	Washington

GEORGIA

001	Appling
003	Atkinson
005	Bacon
007	Baker
009	Baldwin
011	Banks
013	Barrow
015	Bartow

017	Ben Hill	117	Forsyth	217	Newton
019	Berrien	119	Franklin	219	Oconee
021	Bibb	121	Fulton	221	Ogletorpe
023	Bleckley	123	Gilmer	223	Paulding
025	Brantley	125	Glasok	225	Peach
027	Brooks	127	Glynn	227	Pickens
029	Bryan	129	Gordon	229	Pierce
031	Bulloch	131	Grady	231	Pike
033	Burke	133	Greene	233	Polk
035	Butts	135	Gwinnett	235	Pulaski
037	Calhoun	137	Habersham	237	Putnam
039	Camden	139	Hall	239	Quitman
043	Candler	141	Hancock	241	Rabun
045	Carroll	143	Haralson	243	Randolph
047	Cartoosa	145	Harris	245	Richmond
049	Charlton	147	Hart	247	Rockdale
051	Chatham	149	Heard	249	Schley
053	Chattahoochee	151	Henry	251	Screven
055	Chattooga	153	Houston	253	Seminole
057	Cherokee	155	Irwin	255	Spalding
059	Clarke	157	Jackson	257	Stephens
061	Clay	159	Jasper	259	Stewart
063	Clayton	161	Jeff Davis	261	Sumier
065	Clinch	163	Jefferson	263	Talbot
067	Cobb	165	Jenkins	265	Taliaferro
069	Coffee	167	Johnson	267	Tattnall
071	Colquitt	169	Jones	269	Taylor
073	Columbia	171	Lamar	271	Telfair
075	Cook	173	Lanier	273	Terrell
077	Coweta	175	Laurens	275	Thomas
079	Crawford	177	Lee	277	Tift
081	Crisp	179	Liberty	279	Toombs
083	Dade	181	Lincoln	281	Towns
085	Dawson	183	Long	283	Treutlen
087	Decauter	185	Lowndes	285	Troop
089	De Kalb	187	Lumpkin	287	Turner
091	Dodge	189	McDuffie	289	Twiggs
093	Dooly	191	McIntosh	291	Union
095	Dougherty	193	Macon	293	Upson
097	Douglas	195	Madison	295	Walker
099	Early	197	Marion	297	Walton
101	Echols	199	Meriwether	299	Ware
103	Effingham	201	Miller	301	Warren
105	Elbert	205	Mitchell	303	Washington
107	Emanuel	207	Monroe	305	Wayne
109	Evans	209	Montgomery	307	Webster
111	Fannin	211	Morgan	309	Wheeler
113	Fayette	213	Murray	311	White
115	Floyd	215	Muscogee	313	Whitfield

315	Wilcox	063	Lincoln	067	Hancock
317	Wilkes	065	Madison	069	Hardin
319	Wilkinson	067	Minidoka	071	Henderson
321	Worth	069	Nez Perce	073	Henry
		071	Oneida	075	Iroquois

GUAM

		073	Owyhee	077	Jackson
010	Guam	075	Payette	079	Jasper
		077	Power	081	Jefferson
		079	Shoshone	083	Jersey

HAWAII

		081	Teton	085	Jo Daviess
001	Hawaii	083	Twin Falls	087	Johnson
003	Honolulu	085	Valley	089	Kane
007	Kauai	087	Washington	091	Kankakee
009	Maui			093	Kendall

ILLINOIS

IDAHO

		095	Knox		
		097	Lake		
		001	Adams	099	La Salle
001	Ada	003	Alexander	101	Lawrence
003	Adams	005	Bond	103	Lee
005	Bannock	007	Boone	105	Livingston
007	Bear Lake	009	Browne	107	Logan
009	Benewah	011	Bureau	109	Mcdonough
011	Bingham	013	Calhoun	111	McHenry
013	Blaine	015	Carroll	113	McLean
015	Boise	017	Cass	115	Macon
017	Bonner	019	Champaign	117	Macoupin
019	Bonneville	021	Christian	119	Madison
021	Boundary	023	Clark	121	Marion
023	Butte	025	Clay	123	Marshall
025	Camas	027	Clinton	125	Mason
027	Canyon	029	Coles	127	Massac
029	Caribou	031	Cook	129	Menard
031	Cassia	033	Crawford	131	Mercer
033	Clark	035	Cumberland	133	Monroe
035	Clearwater	037	De Kalb	135	Montgomery
037	Custer	039	De Witt	137	Morgan
039	Elmore	041	Douglas	139	Moultrie
041	Franklin	043	Du Page	141	Ogle
043	Fremont	045	Edgar	143	Peoria
045	Gem	047	Edwards	145	Perry
047	Gooding	049	Effingham	147	Piatt
049	Idaho	051	Fayette	149	Pike
051	Jefferson	053	Ford	151	Pope
053	Jerome	055	Franklin	153	Pulaski
055	Kootenai	057	Fulton	155	Putnam
057	Latah	059	Gallatin	157	Randolph
059	Lemhi	061	Green	159	Richland
061	Lewis	063	Grundy	161	Rock Island
		065	Hamilton	163	St. Clair

165	Saline	051	Gibson	149	Starke
167	Sangamon	053	Grant	151	Steuben
169	Shuyler	055	Greene	153	Sullivan
171	Scott	057	Hamilton	155	Switzerland
173	Shelby	059	Hancock	157	Tippecanoe
175	Stark	061	Harrison	159	Tipton
177	Stephenson	063	Hendricks	161	Union
179	Tazewell	065	Henry	163	Vanderburgh
181	Union	067	Howard	165	Vermillion
183	Vermilion	069	Huntington	167	Vigo
185	Wabash	071	Jackson	169	Wabash
187	Warren	073	Jasper	171	Warren
189	Washington	075	Jay	173	Warrick
191	Wayne	077	Jefferson	175	Washington
193	White	079	Jennings	177	Washington
195	Whiteside	081	Johnson	177	Wayne
197	Will	083	Knox	179	Wells
199	Williamson	085	Kosciusko	181	White
201	Winnebago	087	Lagrange	183	Whitley
203	Woodford	089	Lake		
		091	La Porte		
		093	Lawrence		

INDIANA

		095	Madison	**IOWA**	
001	Adams	097	Marion	001	Adair
003	Allen	099	Marshall	003	Adams
005	Bartholomew	101	Martin	005	Allamakee
007	Benton	103	Miami	007	Appanoose
009	Blackford	105	Monroe	009	Audubon
011	Boone	107	Montgomery	011	Benton
013	Brown	109	Morgan	013	Black Hawk
015	Carroll	111	Newton	015	Boone
017	Cass	113	Noble	017	Bremer
019	Clark	115	Ohio	019	Buchanan
021	Clay	117	Orange	021	Buena Vista
023	Clinton	119	Owen	023	Butler
025	Crawford	121	Parke	025	Calhoun
027	Daviess	123	Perry	027	Carroll
029	Dearborn	125	Pike	029	Cass
031	Decatur	127	Porter	031	Cedar
033	De Kalb	129	Posey	033	Cerro Gordo
035	Delaware	131	Pulaski	035	Cherokee
037	Dubois	133	Putnam	037	Chickasaw
039	Elkhart	135	Randolph	039	Clarke
041	Fayette	137	Ripley	041	Clay
043	Floyd	139	Rush	043	Clayton
045	Fountain	141	St. Joseph	045	Clinton
047	Franklin	143	Scott	047	Crawford
049	Fulton	145	Shelby	049	Dallas
		147	Spencer	051	Davis

053	Decatur	153	Polk	047	Edwards
055	Delaware	155	Pottawattamie	049	Elk
057	Des Moines	157	Poweshiek	051	Ellis
059	Dickinson	159	Ringgold	053	Ellsworth
061	Dubuque	161	Sac	055	Finney
063	Emmet	163	Scott	057	Ford
065	Fayette	165	Shelby	059	Franklin
067	Floyd	167	Sioux	061	Geary
069	Franklin	169	Story	063	Gove
071	Fremont	171	Tama	065	Graham
073	Greene	173	Taylor	067	Grant
075	Grundy	175	Union	069	Gray
077	Gutherie	177	Van Buren	071	Greeley
079	Hamilton	179	Wapello	073	Greenwood
081	Hancock	181	Warren	075	Hamilton
083	Hardin	183	Washington	077	Harper
085	Harrison	185	Wayne	079	Harvey
087	Henry	187	Webster	081	Haskell
089	Howard	189	Winnebago	083	Hodgeman
091	Humboldt	191	Winneshiek	085	Jackson
093	Ida	193	Woodbury	087	Jefferson
095	Iowa	195	Worth	089	Jewell
097	Jackson	197	Wright	091	Johnson
099	Jasper			093	Kearny
101	Jefferson	**KANSAS**		095	Kingman
103	Johnson			097	Kiowa
105	Jones	001	Allen	099	Labette
107	Keokuk	003	Anderson	101	Lane
109	Kossuth	005	Atchison	103	Leavenworth
111	Lee	007	Barber	105	Lincoln
113	Linn	009	Barton	107	Linn
115	Louisa	011	Bourbon	109	Logan
117	Lucas	013	Brown	111	Lyon
119	Lyon	015	Butler	113	McPherson
121	Madison	017	Chase	115	Marion
123	Mahaska	019	Chautauqua	117	Marshall
125	Marion	021	Cherokee	119	Meade
127	Marshall	023	Cheyenne	121	Miami
129	Mills	025	Clark	123	Mitchell
131	Mitchell	027	Clay	125	Montgomery
133	Monroe	029	Cloud	127	Morris
137	Montgomery	031	Coffey	129	Morton
139	Muscatine	033	Comanche	131	Nemaha
141	O'Brien	035	Crowley	133	Neosho
143	Osceola	037	Crawford	135	Ness
145	Page	039	Decatur	137	Norton
147	Palo Alto	041	Dickinson	139	Osage
149	Plymouth	043	Doniphan	141	Osborne
151	Pocahontas	045	Douglas	143	Ottawa

145	Pawnee	027	Breckinridge	125	Laurel
147	Phillips	029	Bullitt	127	Lawrence
149	Pottawatomie	031	Butler	129	Lee
151	Pratt	033	Caldwell	131	Leslie
153	Rawlins	035	Calloway	133	Letcher
155	Reno	037	Campbell	135	Lewis
157	Republic	039	Carlisle	137	Lincoln
159	Rice	041	Carroll	139	Livingston
161	Riley	043	Carter	141	Logan
163	Rooks	045	Casey	143	Lyon
165	Rush	047	Christian	145	McCracken
167	Russell	049	Clark	147	McCreary
169	Saline	051	Clay	149	McLean
171	Scott	053	Clinton	151	Madison
173	Sedgwick	055	Crittenden	153	Mgoffin
175	Seward	057	Cumberland	155	Marion
177	Shawnee	059	Daviess	157	Marshall
179	Sheridan	061	Edmonson	159	Martin
181	Sherman	063	Elliott	161	Mason
183	Smith	065	Estill	163	Meade
185	Stafford	067	Fayette	165	Menifee
187	Stanton	069	Fleming	167	Mercer
189	Stevens	071	Floyd	169	Metcalfe
191	Sumner	073	Franklin	171	Monroe
193	Thomas	075	Fulton	173	Montgomery
195	Trego	077	Gallatin	177	Muhlenberg
197	Wabaunsee	079	Garrard	179	Nelson
199	Wallace	081	Grant	181	Nicholas
201	Washington	083	Graves	183	Ohio
203	Wichita	085	Grayson	185	Oldham
205	Wilson	087	Green	187	Owen
207	Woodson	089	Greenup	189	Owsley
209	Wyandette	091	Hancock	191	Pendleton
		093	Hardin	193	Perry
KENTUCKY		095	Harlan	195	Pike
		097	Harrison	197	Powell
001	Adair	099	Hart	199	Polaski
003	Allen	101	Henderson	201	Robertson
005	Anderson	103	Henry	203	Rockcastle
007	Ballard	105	Hickman	205	Rowan
009	Barren	107	Hopkins	207	Russell
011	Bath	109	Jackson	209	Scott
013	Bell	111	Jefferson	211	Shelby
015	Boone	113	Jessamine	213	Simpson
017	Bourbon	115	Johnson	215	Spencer
019	Boyd	117	Kenton	217	Taylor
021	Boyle	119	Knott	219	Todd
023	Bracken	121	Knox	221	Trigg
025	Breathitt	123	Larue	223	Trimble

225	Union
227	Warren
229	Washington
231	Wayne
233	Webster
235	Whiley
237	Wolfe
239	Woodford

LOUISIANA

001	Acadia
003	Allen
005	Ascension
007	Assumption
009	Avoyelles
011	Beauregard
013	Bienville
015	Bossier
017	Caddo
019	Calcasicu
021	Caldwell
023	Cameron
025	Catahoula
027	Claiborne
029	Concordia
031	De Soto
033	East Baton Rouge
035	East Carroll
037	East Feliciana
039	Evangeline
041	Franklin
043	Grant
045	Iberia
047	Iberville
049	Jackson
051	Jefferson
053	Jefferson Davis
055	Lafayette
057	Lafourche
059	La Salle
061	Lincoln
063	Livingston
065	Madison
067	Morehouse
069	Natchitoches
071	Orleans
073	Ouachita

075	Plaquemines
077	Pointe Coupee
079	Rapides
081	Red River
083	Richland
085	Sabine
087	St. Bernard
089	St. Charles
091	St. Helena
093	St. James
095	St. John The Baptist
097	St. Landry
099	St. Martin
101	St. Mary
103	St. Tammany
105	Tangipahoa
107	Tensas
109	Terrebonne
111	Union
113	Vermilion
115	Vernon
117	Washington
119	Webster
121	West Baton Rouge
123	West Carroll
125	West Feliciana
127	Winn

MAINE

001	Androscoggin
003	Aroostook
005	Cumberland
007	Franklin
009	Hancock
011	Kennebec
013	Knox
015	Lincoln
017	Oxford
019	Penobscot
021	Piscataquis
023	Sagadahoc
025	Somerset
027	Waldo
029	Washington
031	York

MARSHALL ISLANDS

007	Ailinginae
010	Ailinglaplap
030	Ailuk
040	Arno
050	Aur
060	Kikar
070	Bikini
073	Bokak
080	Ebon
090	Enewetak
100	Erikub
110	Jabat
120	Jaluit
130	Jemo Island
140	Kili
150	Kwajalein
160	Lae
170	Lib
180	Likiep
190	Majuro
300	Maloelap
310	Mejot
320	Mili
330	Namorik
340	Namu
350	Rongelap
360	Rongrik
385	Toke
390	Ujae
400	Ujelang
410	Utrik
420	Wotho
430	Wotje

MARYLAND

001	Allegany
003	Anne Arundel
510	Baltimore (Independent City)
005	Baltimore (County)
009	Calvert
011	Caroline
013	Carroll
015	Cecil

017	Charles	029	Charlevoix	127	Oceana
019	Dorchester	031	Cheboygan	129	Ogemaw
021	Frederick	033	Chippewa	131	Ontonagon
023	Garrett	035	Clare	133	Oscola
025	Harford	037	Clinton	135	Oscoda
027	Howard	039	Crawford	137	Otsego
029	Kent	041	Delta	139	Ottawa
031	Montgomery	043	Dickinson	141	Presque Isle
033	Prince George's	045	Eaton	143	Roscommon
035	Queen Anne's	047	Emmet	145	Saginaw
039	Somerset	049	Genesee	147	St. Clair
041	Talbot	051	Gladwin	149	St. Joseph
043	Washington	053	Gogebic	151	Sanilac
045	Wicomico	055	Grand Traverse	153	Schoolcraft
047	Worcester	057	Gratiot	155	Shiawassee
		059	Hillsdale	157	Tuscola

MASSACHUSETTS

		061	Houghton	159	Van Buren
		063	Huron	161	Washtenaw
001	Barnstable	065	Ingham	163	Wayne
003	Berkshire	067	Ionia	165	Wexford
005	Bristol	069	Iosco		
007	Dukes	071	Iron		
009	Essex	073	Isabella		
011	Franklin	075	Jackson	**FEDERATED STATES OF**	
013	Hampden	077	Kalamazoo	**MICRONESIA**	
015	Hampshire	079	Kalkaska		
017	Middlesex	081	Kent	005	Kosrae
019	Nantucket	083	Keweenaw	040	Ponape
021	Norfolk	085	Lake	050	Truk
023	Plymouth	087	Lapeer	060	Yap
025	Suffolk	089	Leelanau		
027	Worcester	091	Lenawee		
		093	Livingston	**MINNESOTA**	

MICHIGAN

		095	Luce	001	Aitkin
		097	Mackinac	003	Anoka
001	Alcona	099	Macomb	005	Becker
003	Alger	101	Manistee	007	Beltrami
005	Allegan	103	Marquette	009	Benton
007	Alpena	105	Mason	011	Big Stone
009	Antrim	107	Mecosta	013	Blue Earth
011	Arenac	109	Menominee	015	Brown
013	Baraga	111	Midland	017	Carlton
015	Barry	113	Missaukee	019	Carver
017	Bay	115	Monroe	021	Cass
019	Benzie	117	Montcalm	023	Chippewa
021	Berrien	119	Montmorncy	025	Chicago
023	Branch	121	Muskegon	027	Calay
025	Calhoun	123	Newaygo	029	Clearwater
027	Cass	125	Newyho	031	Cook
				033	Cottonwood
				035	Crow Wing

037	Dakota	135	Roseau	053	Humphrey's
039	Dodge	137	St. Louis	055	Issawuena
041	Douglas	139	Scott	057	Itawamba
043	Faribault	141	Sherburne	059	Jackson
045	Fillmore	143	Sibley	061	Jasper
047	Freeborn	145	Stearns	063	Jefferson
049	Goodhue	147	Steele	065	Jefferson Davis
051	Grant	149	Stevens	067	Jones
053	Hennepin	151	Swift	069	Kemper
055	Houston	153	Todd	071	Lafayette
057	Hubbard	155	Traverse	073	Lamar
059	Isanti	157	Wabasha	075	Lauderdale
061	Itasca	159	Wadena	077	Lawrence
063	Jackson	161	Waseca	079	Leake
065	Kanabee	163	Washington	081	Leake
067	Kandiyohi	165	Watonwan	081	Lee
069	Kittson	167	Wilkin	083	Leflore
071	Koochiching	169	Winona	085	Lincoln
073	Lac Qui Parle	171	Wright	087	Lowndes
075	Lake	173	Yellow Medicine	089	Madison
077	Lake of the Woods			091	Marion
079	Le Sueur	**MISSISSIPPI**		093	Marshall
081	Lincoln			095	Monroe
083	Lyon	001	Adams	097	Montgomery
085	McLeod	003	Alcorn	099	Neshoba
087	Mahnomen	005	Amite	101	Newton
089	Marshall	007	Attala	103	Noxubee
091	Martin	009	Benton	105	Oktibbecha
093	Meeker	011	Bolivar	107	Panola
095	Mille Lacs	013	Calhoun	109	Pearl River
097	Morrison	015	Carroll	111	Perry
099	Mower	017	Chicasaw	113	Pike
101	Murray	019	Choctaw	115	Pontotoc
103	Nicollet	021	Claiborne	117	Prentiss
105	Nobles	023	Clarke	119	Quitman
107	Norman	025	Clay	121	Rankin
109	Olmsted	027	Coahoma	123	Scott
111	Otter Tail	029	Copiah	125	Sharkey
113	Pennington	031	Covington	127	Simpson
115	Pine	033	De Soto	129	Smith
117	Pipestone	035	Forrest	131	Stone
119	Polk	037	Franklin	133	Sunflower
121	Pope	039	George	135	Tallahaichie
123	Ramsey	041	Greene	137	Tate
125	Red Lake	043	Grenada	139	Tippah
127	Redwood	045	Hancock	141	Tishomingo
129	Renville	047	Harrison	143	Tunica
131	Rice	049	Hinds	145	Union
133	Rock	051	Holmes	147	Walthall

149	Warren	077	Greene	175	Randolph
151	Washington	079	Grundy	177	Ray
153	Wayne	081	Harrison	179	Reynolds
155	Webster	083	Henry	181	Ripley
157	Wilkinson	085	Hickory	183	St. Charles
159	Winston	087	Holt	185	St. Clair
161	Yalobusha	089	Howard	186	Ste. Genevieve
163	Yazoo	091	Howell	187	St. Francois
		093	Iron	189	St. Louis (County)
MISSOURI		095	Jackson	510	St. Louis (Independent City)
		097	Jasper		
001	Adair	099	Jefferson	195	Saline
003	Andrew	101	Johnson	197	Schuyler
005	Atchinson	103	Knox	199	Scotland
007	Audrain	105	Laclede	201	Scott
009	Barry	107	Lafayette	203	Shannon
011	Barton	109	Lawrence	205	Shelby
013	Bates	111	Lewis	207	Stoddard
015	Benton	113	Lincoln	209	Stone
017	Bollinger	115	Linn	211	Sullivan
019	Boone	117	Livingston	213	Taney
021	Buchanan	119	McDonald	215	Texas
023	Butler	121	Macon	217	Vernon
025	Caldwell	123	Madison	219	Warren
027	Callaway	125	Maries	221	Washington
029	Camden	127	Marion	223	Wayne
031	Cape Girardeau	129	Mercer	225	Webster
033	Carroll	131	Miller	227	Worth
035	Carter	133	Mississippi	229	Wright
037	Cass	135	Moniteau		
039	Cedar	137	Monroe	**MONTANA**	
041	Chariton	139	Montgomery		
043	Christian	141	Morgan	001	Beaverhead
045	Clark	143	New Madrid	003	Big Horn
047	Clay	145	Newton	005	Blaine
049	Clinton	147	Nodaway	007	Broadwater
051	Cole	149	Oregon	009	Carbon
053	Cooper	151	Osage	011	Carter
055	Crawford	153	Ozark	013	Cascade
057	Dade	155	Pemiscot	015	Chouteau
059	Dallas	157	Perry	017	Custer
061	Daviess	159	Pettis	019	Daniels
063	De Kalb	161	Phelps	021	Dawson
065	Dent	163	Pike	023	Deer Lodge
067	Douglas	165	Platte	025	Fallon
069	Dunklin	167	Polk	027	Fergus
071	Franklin	169	Pulaski	029	Flathead
073	Gasonade	171	Putnam	031	Gallatin
075	Gentry	173	Ralls	033	Garfield

035	Glacier	013	Box Butte	111	Lincoln
037	Golden Valley	015	Boyd	113	Logan
039	Granite	017	Brown	115	Loup
041	Hill	019	Buffalo	117	McPherson
043	Jefferson	021	Burt	119	Madison
045	Judith Basin	023	Butler	121	Merrick
047	Lake	025	Cass	123	Merill
049	Lewis and Clark	027	Cedar	125	Nance
051	Liberty	029	Chase	127	Nemaha
053	Lincoln	031	Cherry	129	Nuckolls
055	McCone	033	Cheyenne	131	Otoe
057	Madison	035	Clay	133	Pawnee
059	Meagher	037	Colfax	135	Perkins
061	Mineral	039	Cuming	137	Phelps
063	Missoula	041	Custer	139	Pierce
065	Musselshell	043	Dakota	141	Platte
067	Park	045	Dawes	143	Polk
069	Petroleum	047	Dawson	145	Red Willow
071	Phillips	049	Deuel	147	Richardson
073	Pondera	051	Dixon	149	Rok
075	Powder River	053	Dodge	151	Saline
077	Powell	055	Douglas	153	Sarpy
079	Prairie	057	Dundy	155	Saunders
081	Ravalli	059	Fillmore	157	Scotts Bluff
083	Richland	061	Franklin	159	Seward
085	Roosevelt	063	Frontier	161	Sheridan
087	Rosebud	065	Furnas	163	Sherman
089	Sanders	067	Gage	165	Sioux
091	Sheridan	069	Garden	167	Stanton
093	Silver Bow	071	Garfield	169	Thayer
095	Stillwater	073	Gosper	171	Thomas
097	Sweet Grass	075	Grant	173	Thurston
099	Teton	077	Greeley	175	Valley
101	Toole	079	Hall	177	Washington
103	Treasure	081	Hamilton	179	Wayne
105	Valley	083	Harlan	181	Webster
107	Wheatland	085	Hayes	183	Wheeler
109	Wibaux	087	Hitchcock	185	York
111	Yellowstone	089	Holt		
113	Yellowstone Nat Park	091	Hooker		
		093	Howard	**NEVADA**	

NEBRASKA

		095	Jefferson	001	Churchill
		097	Johnson	003	Clark
001	Adama	099	Kearney	005	Douglas
003	Antelope	101	Keith	007	Elko
005	Arthur	103	Keya Paha	009	Esmeralda
007	Banner	105	Kimball	011	Eureka
009	Blaine	107	Knox	013	Humboldt
011	Boone	109	Lancaster	015	Lander

		NEW MEXICO			
017	Lincoln			023	Cortland
019	Lyon	001	Bernalillo	025	Delaware
021	Mineral	003	Catron	027	Duchess
023	Nye	005	Chaves	029	Eric
027	Pershing	006	Cibola	031	Essex
029	Storey	007	Colfax	033	Franklin
031	Washoe	009	Curry	035	Fulton
033	White Plain	011	De Baca	037	Genesee
510	Carson City	013	Dona Ana	039	Greene
		015	Eddy	041	Hamilton
NEW HAMPSHIRE		017	Grant	043	Herkimer
		019	Guadalupe	045	Jefferson
001	Belknap	021	Harding	047	Kings
003	Carroll	023	Hidalgo	049	Lewis
005	Cheshire	025	Lea	051	Livingston
007	Coos	027	Lincoln	053	Madison
009	Grafton	028	Los Alamos	055	Monroe
011	Hillsborough	029	Luna	057	Montgomery
013	Merrimack	031	McKinley	059	Nassau
015	Rockingham	033	Mora	061	New York
017	Strafford	035	Otero	063	Niagara
019	Sullivan	037	Quay	065	Oneida
		039	Rio Arriba	067	Onondaga
NEW JERSEY		041	Roosevelt	069	Ontario
		043	Sandoval	071	Orange
001	Atlantic	045	San Juan	073	Orleans
003	Bergen	047	San Miguel	075	Oswego
005	Burlington	049	Santa Fe	077	Oisego
007	Camden	051	Sierra	079	Putnam
009	Cape May	053	Socorro	081	Queens
011	Cumberland	055	Taos	083	Rensselaer
013	Essex	057	Torrance	085	Richmond
015	Gloucester	059	Union	087	Rockland
017	Hudson	061	Valencia	089	St. Lawrence
019	Hunterdon			091	Saratoga
021	Mercer	**NEW YORK**		093	Schenectady
023	Middlesex			095	Schoharic
025	Monmouth	001	Albany	097	Schuyler
027	Morris	003	Allegany	099	Seneca
029	Ocean	005	Bronx	101	Steuben
031	Passaic	007	Broome	103	Suffolk
033	Salem	009	Cattaraugus	105	Sullivan
035	Somerset	011	Cayuga	107	Tioga
037	Sussex	013	Chautauqua	109	Tompkins
039	Union	015	Chemung	111	Ultster
041	Warren	017	Chenango	113	Warren
		019	Clinton	115	Washington
		021	Columbia		

117	Wayne	085	Haywood	185	Warren
119	Westchester	089	Henderson	187	Washington
121	Wyoming	091	Hertford	189	Waauga
123	Yates	093	Hoke	191	Wayne
		095	Hyde	193	Wilkes
NORTH CAROLINA		097	Iredell	195	Wilson
		099	Jackson	197	Yadkin
001	Alamance	101	Johnston	199	Yancey
003	Alexander	103	Jones		
005	Alleghany	105	Lee	**NORTH DAKOTA**	
007	Anson	107	Lenoir		
009	Ashe	109	Lincoln	001	Adams
011	Avery	111	McDowell	003	Barnes
013	Beaufort	113	Macon	005	Benson
015	Bertie	115	Madison	007	Billings
017	Bladen	117	Martin	009	Bottineau
019	Brunswick	119	Mecklenberg	011	Bowman
021	Buncombe	121	Mitchell	013	Burke
023	Burke	123	Montgomery	015	Burleigh
025	Cabarrus	125	Moore	017	Cass
027	Caldwell	127	Nash	019	Cavalier
029	Camden	129	New Hanover	021	Dickey
031	Carteret	131	Northampton	023	Divide
033	Caswell	133	Onslow	025	Dunn
035	Catawba	135	Orange	027	Eddy
037	Chatham	137	Pamlico	029	Emmons
039	Cherokee	139	Pasquotank	031	Foster
041	Chowan	141	Pender	033	Golden Valley
043	Clay	143	Perquimans	035	Grand Forks
045	Cleveland	145	Person	037	Grant
047	Columbus	147	Pitt	039	Griggs
049	Craven	149	Polk	041	Hettinger
051	Cumberland	151	Randolph	043	Kidder
053	Currituck	153	Richmond	045	La Moure
055	Dare	155	Robeson	047	Logan
057	Davidson	157	Rockingham	049	McHenry
059	Davie	159	Rowan	051	McIntosh
061	Duplin	161	Rutherford	053	McKenzie
063	Durham	163	Sampson	055	McLean
065	Edgecombe	165	Scotland	057	Mercer
067	Forsyth	167	Stanley	059	Morton
069	Franklin	169	Stokes	061	Mountrail
071	Gaston	171	Surrey	063	Nelson
073	Gates	173	Swain	065	Oliver
075	Graham	175	Transylvania	067	Pembina
077	Granville	177	Tyrrell	069	Pierce
079	Greene	179	Union	071	Ramsey
081	Guilford	181	Vance	073	Ranson
083	Halifax	183	Wake	075	Renville

077	Richland	049	Franklin	147	Seneca
079	Rolette	051	Fulton	149	Shelby
081	Sargent	053	Gallia	151	Stark
083	Sheridan	055	Geauga	153	Summit
085	Sioux	057	Greene	155	Trumbull
087	Slope	059	Guernsey	157	Tuscarawas
089	Stark	061	Hamilton	159	Union
091	Steele	063	Hancock	161	Van Wert
093	Stutsman	065	Hardin	163	Vinton
095	Towner	067	Harrison	165	Warren
097	Trail	069	Henry	167	Washington
099	Walsh	071	Highland	169	Wayne
101	Ward	073	Hocking	171	Williams
103	Wells	075	Holmes	173	Wood
105	Williams	077	Huron	175	Wyandot
		079	Jackson		

NORTHERN MARIANAS

085	Northern Islands
100	Rota
110	Saipan
120	Tinian

OHIO

		081	Jefferson		
		083	Knox		
001	Adams	085	Lake		
003	Allen	087	Lawrence		
005	Ashland	089	Licking	**OKLAHOMA**	
007	Ashtabula	091	Logan		
009	Athens	093	Lorain	001	Adair
011	Auglaize	095	Lucas	003	Alfalfa
013	Belmont	097	Madison	005	Atoka
015	Brown	099	Mahoning	007	Beaver
017	Butler	101	Marion	009	Beckham
019	Carroll	103	Medina	011	Blaine
021	Champaign	105	Meigs	013	Bryan
023	Clark	107	Mercer	015	Caddo
025	Clermont	109	Miami	017	Canadian
027	Clinton	111	Monroe	019	Carter
029	Columbiana	113	Montgomery	021	Cherokee
031	Coshocton	115	Morgan	023	Choctaw
033	Crawford	117	Murrow	025	Cimarron
035	Cuyahoga	119	Muskingum	027	Cleveland
037	Darke	121	Noble	029	Coal
039	Defiance	123	Ottawa	031	Commanche
041	Delaware	125	Paulding	033	Cotton
043	Erie	127	Perry	035	Craig
045	Fairfield	129	Pickaway	037	Creek
047	Fayette	131	Pike	039	Custer
		133	Portage	041	Delaware
		135	Preble	043	Dewey
		137	Putnam	045	Ellis
		139	Richland	047	Garfield
		141	Ross	049	Garvin
		143	Sandusky	051	Grady
		145	Scioto	053	Grant
				055	Greer
				057	Harmon
				059	Harper
				061	Haskell

063	Hughes			218	Ngarchelong
065	Jackson	**OREGON**		222	Ngardmau
067	Jefferson			223	Ngaremlengui
069	Johnston	001	Baker	224	Ngatpang
071	Kay	003	Benton	226	Ngehesar
073	Kingfisher	005	Clackamas	228	Ngiwai
075	Kiowa	007	Clatsop	300	Palau-unorg
077	Latimer	009	Columbia	350	Peleliu
079	Le Flore	011	Coos	370	Sonsorol
081	Lincoln	013	Crook	380	Tobi
083	Logan	015	Curry		
085	Love	017	Deschutes	**PENNSYLVANIA**	
087	McClain	019	Douglas		
089	McCurtain	021	Gilliam	001	Adams
091	McIntosh	023	Grant	003	Allegheny
093	Major	025	Harney	005	Armstrong
095	Marshall	027	Hood River	007	Beaver
097	Mayes	029	Jackson	009	Bedford
099	Murray	031	Jefferson	011	Berks
101	Muskogee	033	Josephine	013	Blair
103	Noble	035	Klamath	015	Bradford
105	Nowata	037	Lake	017	Bucks
107	Okfuskee	039	Lane	019	Butler
109	Oklahoma	041	Lincoln	021	Cambria
111	Okmulgee	043	Linn	023	Cameron
113	Osage	045	Malheur	025	Carbon
115	Ottawa	047	Marion	027	Centre
117	Pawnee	049	Morrow	029	Chester
119	Payne	051	Multnomah	031	Clarion
121	Pittsburg	053	Polk	033	Clearfield
123	Pontotoc	055	Sherman	035	Clinton
125	Pottawatomie	057	Tillamook	037	Columbia
127	Pushmataha	059	Umatilla	039	Crawford
129	Roger Mills	061	Union	041	Cumberland
131	Rogers	063	Wallowa	043	Dauphin
133	Seminole	065	Wasco	045	Delaware
135	Sequoyah	067	Washington	047	Elk
137	Stephens	069	Wheeler	049	Erie
139	Texas	071	Yamhill	051	Fayette
141	Tillman			053	Forest
143	Tulsa	**PALAU**		055	Franklin
145	Wagoner			057	Fulton
147	Washington	002	Aimeliik	059	Greene
149	Washita	004	Airai	061	Huntingdon
151	Woods	010	Angaur	063	Indiana
153	Woodward	100	Kayangel	065	Jefferson
		150	Koror	067	Juniata
		212	Melekeiok	069	Lackawanna
		214	Ngaraard	071	Lancaster

073	Lawrence	031	Carolina	121	Sabana Grande
075	Lebanon	025	Caguas	123	Salinas
077	Lehigh	029	Canovanas	125	San German
079	Luzerne	031	Carolina	127	San Juan
081	Lycoming	033	Catano	129	San Lorenzo
083	McKean	035	Cayey	131	San Sebastian
085	Mercer	037	Ceiba	133	Santa Isabel
087	Mifflin	039	Ciales	135	Toa Alta
089	Monroe	041	Cidra	137	Toabaja
091	Montgomery	043	Coamo	139	Trujillo alto
093	Montour	045	Comerio	141	Utuado
095	Northampton	047	Corozal	143	Vega Alta
097	Northumberland	049	Culebra	145	Vega Baja
099	Perry	051	Dorado	147	Vieques
101	Philadelphia	053	Fajardo	149	Villalba
103	Pike	054	Florida	151	Yabucoa
105	Potter	055	Guanica	153	Yauco
107	Schuylkill	057	Guayama		
109	Snyder	059	Guayanilla	**RHODE ISLAND**	
111	Somerset	061	Guaynabo		
113	Sullivan	063	Gurabo	001	Bristol
115	Susquehanna	065	Hatillo	003	Kent
117	Tioga	067	Hormigueros	005	Newport
119	Union	069	Humacao	007	Providence
121	Venango	071	Isabela	009	Washington
123	Warren	073	Jayuya		
125	Washington	075	Juana Diaz	**SOUTH CAROLINA**	
127	Wayne	077	Juncos		
129	Westmoreland	079	Lajas	001	Abbeville
131	Wyoming	081	Lares	003	Aiken
133	York	083	Las Marias	005	Allendale
		085	Las Piedras	007	Anderson
PUERTO RICO		087	Loiza	009	Bamberg
		089	Luquillo	011	Barnwell
001	Adjuntas	091	Manati	013	Beaufort
003	Aguada	093	Maricao	015	Berkeley
005	Aguadilla	095	Maunabo	017	Calhoun
007	Aguas Buenas	097	Mayaguez	019	Charleston
009	Aibinito	099	Moca	021	Cherokee
011	Anasco	101	Morovis	023	Chester
013	Arecibo	103	Naguabo	025	Chesterfield
015	Arroyo	105	Naranjito	027	Clarendon
017	Barceloneta	107	Orocovis	029	Colleton
019	Barranquitas	109	Patillas	031	Darlington
021	Bayamon	111	Penuelas	033	Dillon
023	Cabo Rojo	113	Ponce	035	Dorchester
025	Caguas	115	Quebradillas	037	Edgefield
027	Camuy	117	Rincon	039	Fairfield
029	Canovanas	119	Rio Grande	041	Florence

102

043	Georgetown	045	Edmunds	**TENNESSEE**	
045	Greenville	047	Fall River		
047	Greenood	049	Faulk	001	Anderson
049	Hampton	051	Grant	003	Bedford
051	Horry	053	Gregory	005	Benton
053	Jasper	055	Haakon	007	Bledsoe
055	Kershaw	057	Hamlin	009	Blount
057	Lancaster	059	Hand	011	Bradley
059	Laurens	061	Hanson	013	Campbell
061	Lee	063	Harding	015	Cannon
063	Lexington	065	Hughes	017	Carroll
065	McCormick	067	Hutchinson	019	Carter
067	Marion	069	Hyde	021	Cheatham
069	Marlboro	071	Jackson	023	Chester
071	Newberry	073	Jerauld	025	Claiborne
073	Ocanee	075	Jones	027	Clay
075	Orangeburg	077	Kingsbury	029	Cocke
077	Pickens	079	Lake	031	Coffee
079	Richland	081	Lawrence	033	Crockett
081	Saluda	083	Lincoln	035	Cumberland
083	Spartanburg	085	Lyman	037	Davidson
085	Sumter	087	McCook	039	Decatur
087	Union	089	McPherson	041	De Kalb
089	Williamsburg	091	Marshall	043	Dickson
091	York	093	Meade	045	Dyer
		095	Mellette	047	Fayette
SOUTH DAKOTA		097	Miner	049	Fentress
		099	Minnehaha	051	Franklin
003	Aurora	101	Moody	053	Gibson
005	Beadle	103	Pennington	055	Giles
007	Bennett	105	Perkins	057	Grainger
009	Bon Homme	107	Potter	059	Greene
011	Brookings	109	Roberts	061	Grundy
013	Brown	111	Sanborn	063	Hamblen
015	Brule	113	Shannon	065	Hamilton
017	Buffalo	115	Spink	067	Hancock
019	Butte	117	Stanley	069	Hardeman
021	Campbell	119	Sully	071	Hardin
023	Charles Mix	121	Todd	073	Hawkins
025	Clark	123	Tripp	075	Haywood
027	Clay	125	Turner	077	Henderson
029	Codington	127	Union	079	Henry
031	Corson	129	Walworth	081	Hickman
033	Custer	135	Yankton	083	Houston
035	Davison	137	Ziebach	085	Humphreys
037	Day			087	Jackson
039	Deuel			089	Jefferson
041	Dewey			091	Johnson
043	Douglas			093	Knox

095	Lake	**TEXAS**		095	Concho
097	Lauderdale			097	Cooke
099	Lawrence	001	Anderson	099	Coryell
101	Lewis	003	Andrews	101	Cottle
103	Lincoln	005	Angelina	103	Crane
105	Loudon	007	Aransas	105	Crockett
107	McMinn	009	Archer	107	Crosby
109	McNairy	011	Armstrong	109	Culberson
111	Macon	013	Atascosa	111	Dallam
113	Madison	015	Austin	113	Dallas
115	Marion	017	Bailey	115	Dawson
117	Marshall	019	Bandera	117	Deaf Smith
119	Maury	021	Bastrop	119	Delta
121	Meigs	023	Baylor	121	Denton
123	Monroe	025	Bee	123	De Witt
125	Montgomery	027	Bell	125	Dickens
127	Moore	029	Bexar	127	Dimmit
129	Morgan	031	Blanco	129	Donley
131	Overton	033	Bordon	131	Duval
135	Perry	035	Bosque	133	Eastland
137	Pickett	037	Bowie	135	Ector
139	Polk	039	Brazoria	137	Edwards
141	Putnam	041	Brazos	139	Ellis
143	Rhea	043	Brewster	141	El Paso
145	Roane	045	Briscoe	143	Erath
147	Robertson	047	Brooks	145	Falls
149	Rutherford	049	Brown	147	Fannin
151	Scott	051	Burleson	149	Fayette
153	Sequatchie	053	Burnet	151	Fisher
155	Sevier	055	Caldwell	153	Floyd
157	Shelby	057	Calhoun	155	Foard
159	Smith	059	Callahan	157	Fort Bend
161	Stewart	061	Cameron	159	Franklin
163	Sullivan	063	Camp	161	Freestone
165	Sumner	065	Carson	163	Frio
167	Tipton	067	Cass	165	Gaines
169	Trousdale	069	Castro	167	Galveston
171	Unicoi	071	Chambers	169	Garza
173	Union	073	Cherokee	171	Gillespie
175	Van Buren	075	Childress	173	Glasscock
177	Warren	077	Clay	175	Goliad
179	Washington	079	Cochran	177	Gonzales
181	Wayne	081	Coke	179	Gray
183	Weakley	083	Coleman	181	Grayson
185	White	085	Collin	183	Gregg
187	Williamson	087	Collingsworth	185	Grimes
189	Wilson	089	Colorado	187	Guadalupe
		091	Comal	189	Hale
		093	Comanche	191	Hall

Suggested Readings

Bluemenson, John J.G.
*Identifying American
Architecture: A Pictorial Guide to
Styles and Terms, 1600-1945*
Norton Publishing, New York,198

Gillon Jr., Edmund V. and Clay Lancaster
*Victorian Houses: A Treasury of Lesser-
Known Examples*
Dover Publications Inc., New York, 1973

Greene, Fayal and Bonita Bavetta
The Anatomy of a House

Hamlin, Talbot.
Greek Revival Architecture in America
Dover Publications, New York, 1964 reprint

Harris, Cyril M., ed.
*Illustrated Dictionary of Historic
Architecture*
Dover Publications, Inc., New York, 1977

Kidney, Walter C.
*The Architecture of Choice: Eclecticism in
America 1880-1930*
George Braziller, New York, 1974

Lancaster, Clay.
The American Bungalow, 1880-1930
Abbeville Press, New York, 1985.

Maddex, Diane, ed.
*Master Builders: A Guide to Famous
American Architects*
The National Trust for Historic Preservation,
Washington, DC., 1985

O'Gorman, James F.
The Architecture of Frank Furness
The Philadelphia Museum of Art,
Philadelphia, 1973

Placzek, Adolph K. Editor in Chief
Macmillan Encyclopedia of Architects
Free Pass, 1982
4 Volumes with Index

Poppeliers, John C., et al.
What Style Is It?
The National Trust for Historic
Preservation, Washington DC., 1983

Preservation Press
*The Culture Vulture:
A Guide to Style, Period and Ism.*
Paperback

Rifkind, Carole
*A Field Guide to American
Architecture*
New American Library, New
York, 1980

Roth, Leland M.
*A Concise History of American
Architecture*
Harper & Row, New York, 1979

Scully, Vincent
The Shingle Style Today
George Braziller, New York, 1974

Sloan, Samuel
Sloan's Victorian Buildings
Dover Publications, New York, 1980

Smith, Kidder G.E..*The Architecture
of the United States*
3 volumes An Illustrated 3 volume
guide.
Vol. 1: New England and the Mid-
Atlantic States;
Vol. 2: The South and the Midwest;
Vol. 3: The Plains States and Far West
Doubleday/Anchor Books, New York,
1981

Stevenson, Katherine Cole & H.
Ward Jandl..
*Houses by Mail; A Guide to Houses
from Sears, Roebuck and Company*
National Trust for Historic
Preservation, Washington DC., 1986

Stickley, Gustav
*Craftsman Homes: Architecture
and Furnishings of the American
Arts and Crafts Movement*
Dover Publications, New York,1979

Whiffen, Marcus
*American Architecture Since
1780: A Guide To The Styles.*
MIT Press, Cambridge, 1969

Sample

Application

Form

OMB No. 10024-0018

SAMPLE

United States Department of the Interior
National Park Service

National Register of Historic Places Registration Form

This form is for use in nominating or requesting determinations for individual properties and districts. See instructions in *How to Complete the National Register of Historic Places Registration Form* (National Register Bulletin 16A). Complete each item by marking "x" in the appropriate box or by entering the information requested. If an item does not apply to the property being documented, enter "N/A" for "not applicable." For functions, architectural classification, materials, and areas of significance, enter only categories and subcategories from the instructions. Place additional entries and narrative items on continuation sheets (NPS Form 10-900a). Use a typewriter, word processor, or computer, to complete all items.

1. Name of Property

historic name ___Peter Mott house___

other names/site number _____

2. Location

street & number _Moore Avenue at Gloucester Avenue_ ☐ not for publication

city or town __Lawnside Borough__ ☐ vicinity

state _New Jersey_ code _034_ county _Camden_ code _007_ zip code _08045_

3. State/Federal Agency Certification

As the designated authority under the National Historic Preservation Act, as amended, I hereby certify that this ☐ nomination ☐ request for determination of eligibility meets the documentation standards for registering properties in the National Register of Historic Places and meets the procedural and professional requirements set forth in 36 CFR Part 60. In my opinion, the property ☐ meets ☐ does not meet the National Register criteria. I recommend that this property be considered significant ☐ nationally ☐ statewide ☐ locally. (☐ See continuation sheet for additional comments.)

_____
Signature of certifying official/Title   Date

_____
State of Federal agency and bureau

In my opinion, the property ☐ meets ☐ does not meet the National Register criteria. (☐ See continuation sheet for additional comments.)

_____
Signature of certifying official/Title   Date

_____
State or Federal agency and bureau

4. National Park Service Certification

I hereby certify that the property is:

☐ entered in the National Register.
   ☐ See continuation sheet.
☐ determined eligible for the National Register
   ☐ See continuation sheet.
☐ determined not eligible for the National Register.
☐ removed from the National Register.
☐ other, (explain:) _____

Signature of the Keeper   Date of Action

_____

_____

_____

_____

Peter Mott house
Name of Property

Camden Co., NJ
County and State

5. Classification

Ownership of Property
(Check as many boxes as apply)

- ☒ private
- ☐ public-local
- ☐ public-State
- ☐ public-Federal

Category of Property
(Check only one box)

- ☒ building(s)
- ☐ district
- ☐ site
- ☐ structure
- ☐ object

Number of Resources within Property
(Do not include previously listed resources in the count.)

Contributing	Noncontributing	
1	0	buildings
		sites
		structures
		objects
1	0	Total

Name of related multiple property listing
(Enter "N/A" if property is not part of a multiple property listing.)

N/A

Number of contributing resources previously listed in the National Register

0

6. Function or Use

Historic Functions
(Enter categories from instructions)

DOMESTIC/single dwelling

Current Functions
(Enter categories from instructions)

WORK IN PROGRESS

7. Description

Architectural Classification
(Enter categories from instructions)

Mid-19th Century

Materials
(Enter categories from instructions)

foundation   Brick, stone

walls asphalt

shingle

roof   asphalt

other

Narrative Description
(Describe the historic and current condition of the property on one or more continuation sheets.)

113

United States Department of the Interior
National Park Service

National Register of Historic Places
Continuation Sheet

Section number ___7___   Page ___1___

THE PETER MOTT HOUSE
LAWNSIDE, CAMDEN COUNTY, NJ

NARRATIVE DESCRIPTION: ARCHITECTURAL

The Peter Mott House located within the King's Court subdivision of the Borough of Lawnside, NJ, [Photo #1] is in close proximity to Interstate Route 295, the New Jersey Turnpike and the White Horse Pike. Oriented toward the latter road, it is a small, rectangular, two story wood frame structure, one room deep, with a gable roof, approximately 15' by 40' in plan. Built in two stages, c.1845 and c.1870,[1] the older section has a full basement with brick and rubble stone masonry foundation walls; the newer section has only a shallow crawl space and brick masonry foundation of unknown depth. The Mott House is the oldest known house in the borough. The older part of the building is on the south; the later one-room addition maintains the lines of the original house. The interior of the house reflects the simplicity of its exterior. The overall building condition is poor but stabilized.

The exterior fabric of the gable-roofed house consists of asphalt roofing shingles over wood shingles [#2] and asphalt wall shingles (east face) [# 3] over wood shingles atop the original clapboard. Six-over-six sash single-hung windows, originally shuttered, punctuate the walls and a five-panel entrance door is centered on the west facade. A simple box cornice runs the length of both east and west walls and a single-flue stuccoed brick chimney extends above the ridge line. The roof framing consists of a single gable of simple rafters; in the older portion they meet at the ridge in a pegged mortise-and-tenon connection; in the newer portion they are mitred and nailed together.

---

[1]Westfield Architects & Preservation Consultants, The Peter Mott House: Preservation Plan & Feasibility Study (Haddon Hts., July 1992), p. 7.

114

NPS Form 10-900-a
(8-86)

OMB Approval No. 1024-0018

United States Department of the Interior
National Park Service

National Register of Historic Places
Continuation Sheet

Section number ___7___   Page ___2___

THE PETER MOTT HOUSE
LAWNSIDE, CAMDEN COUNTY, NJ

The older part of the building features a full basement, first
floor parlor, two second floor bedrooms and a fenestrated attic.
The one-room wide north addition maintains the lines of the
original house but was built over a shallow crawlspace. All the
floor and roof framing members span in the east-west direction and
bear on the front and rear walls of the building. A framed-out
opening at the south end of the basement exhibits pegged mortise-
and-tenon connections probably contemporary with the original
framing.

Subsequent alterations have included substitution of deeper
joists and beams inside the east and west foundation walls to re-
support rotted joist ends. Second floor framing, also probably in
its original configuration is composed of 3" x 6" joists, 24" on
center spanning the entire 15' depth of the building.

The first-floor plan consists of two rooms separated by a
narrow stair. The original "south" room contains a beaded
baseboard, evidence of a two-piece molded chair rail, and simple
door and window trim. The room has a window on the east and south
walls and a window and door on the west wall. The walls and ceiling
are plastered; the wood floor boards painted. A board-and-batten
door to the basement retains 19th century hardware. The "north"
room [# 4 & 5] has one window on the west wall, one window on the
north wall and a door on the east wall. A built-in cupboard,
contemporary with the addition (c. 1870), has survived in the
southeast corner of the "north" room.

The second floor is divided into three rooms and a stair. The
room to the south is square and contains a window in the west and
east walls. The middle room, adjacent to the stair, also has one
window in each of the east and west walls. This room was converted
into a bathroom and has a bathtub, toilet, sink and small closet.
The north/addition room [#6] has one window in each of the east and
west walls.

NPS Form 10-900-a
(8-86)

United States Department of the Interior
National Park Service

National Register of Historic Places
Continuation Sheet

Section number __7__   Page __3__

THE PETER MOTT HOUSE
LAWNSIDE, CAMDEN COUNTY, NJ

Access to the attic is through a winding stair entered from the
bathroom. The attic space is unfinished although insulated.
The south gable end wall is punctuated with a 4/4 single-hung window. All
structure is exposed and mortise-and-tenon joinery is used at the ridge on the
south end of the house. [#7] A brick chimney adjoins the original end wall
framing. The rafters of the south addition are joined with cut nails. The
exposed roof framing reveals second generation cedar shingles above spaced
roof lath.

The basement located under the original portion of the house has a dirt
floor; three foundation walls are of brick, one foundation wall is composed of
stone and brick. Stonework on the north wall provides evidence of the past
existence of a fireplace vault. The joists span from east to west with a
central girder. Although an interior stairway once existed, at present access
is only through an exterior bulkhead opening.

Vacant and neglected since the death of its last occupant in 1987, the
property on which the Peter Mott House stands was purchased and subdivided by
a local developer who erected 20 semi-detached homes and planned to demolish
the Mott House. Local residents united to prevent demolition, incorporated as
the Lawnside Historical Society and secured funding for a feasibility study by
Westfield Architects of Haddon Heights, New Jersey. Finally, the developer
donated the house to the Historical Society for a museum.

While the overall condition of the building is poor; it has been
stabilized for the time being and a preservation plan has been developed for
the Lawnside Historical Society; a condition survey is to be completed by
November, 1993 and an archaeological survey will be done before there is
further disturbance of the ground.

8. Statement of Significance

Applicable National Register Criteria
(Mark "x" in one or more boxes for the criteria qualifying the property for National Register listing.)

☒ A Property is associated with events that have made a significant contribution to the broad patterns of our history.

☒ B Property is associated with the lives of persons significant in our past.

☒ C Property embodies the distinctive characteristics of a type, period, or method of construction or represents the work of a master, or possesses high artistic values, or represents a significant and distinguishable entity whose components lack individual distinction.

☐ D Property has yielded, or is likely to yield, information important in prehistory or history.

Criteria Considerations
(Mark "x" in all the boxes that apply.)

Property is:

☐ A owned by a religious institution or used for religious purposes.

☐ B removed from its original location.

☐ C a birthplace or grave.

☐ D a cemetery.

☐ E a reconstructed building, object, or structure.

☐ F a commemorative property.

☐ G less than 50 years of age or achieved significance within the past 50 years.

Areas of Significance
(Enter categories from instructions)

Ethnic Heritage: Black

Social History

Architecture

Period of Significance

Ca.1845 - 1879

Significant Dates

Ca.1845

Ca.1870

Significant Person
(Complete if Criterion B is marked above)

Mott, Peter (1807?-1881)

Cultural Affiliation

N/A

Architect/Builder

Unknown

Narrative Statement of Significance
(Explain the significance of the property on one or more continuation sheets.)

9. Major Bibliographical References

Bibilography
(Cite the books, articles, and other sources used in preparing this form on one or more continuation sheets.)

Previous documentation on file (NPS):

☐ preliminary determination of individual listing (36 CFR 67) has been requested
☐ previously listed in the National Register
☐ previously determined eligible by the National Register
☐ designated a National Historic Landmark
☐ recorded by Historic American Buildings Survey
  # _____
☐ recorded by Historic American Engineering
  Record # _____

Primary location of additional data:

☐ State Historic Preservation Office
☐ Other State agency
☐ Federal agency
☒ Local government
☐ University
☐ Other

Name of repository:

Camden County Cultural & Heritage Comm.

United States Department of the Interior
National Park Service

National Register of Historic Places
Continuation Sheet

Section number __8__   Page _4___

THE PETER MOTT HOUSE
LAWNSIDE, CAMDEN COUNTY, N.J.

STATEMENT OF SIGNIFICANCE:

The Peter Mott House is a rare surviving example of a housing type associated with the early development of Lawnside, the only ante-bellum African-American community to later become an incorporated municipality in the State of New Jersey.

The house was the residence of Peter Mott (c. 1807 ? - 1881) between c. 1844 when he acquired the first of three parcels of land on which it was erected and 1879 when he sold it to Levis Moore; it was here on a tract of land previously owned by Jacob C. White, Sr., a black Philadelphian prominent in the Underground Railroad movement,[2] that, according to impressive circumstantial evidence and oral testimony, Mott and his wife, Elizabeth Ann Thomas, lived and provided sanctuary to runaway slaves. Mott, a free black farmer, also served as a minister at Snow Hill Church.[3] He founded its Sunday School in 1847, becoming the first Superintendent of what is the second oldest African-American Sunday School in the area[4], organized c. 1792. Today it is known as the Mount Pisgah African Methodist Episocpal Church. The Peter Mott House meets National Register Criterion B for its association with Mott, an important early settler in Snow Hill, **Criterion C** as a rare example of an ante-bellum black landowner's home in Snow Hill and, Criterion A for a property associated with the Underground Railroad. Forceful circumstantial evidence, and oral traditions within the borough of Lawnside strongly suggest that Mott was involved with Underground Railroad activities and used his home as a "station".

---

[2]Ms# 1699, Orrin Evans, "An Account of several Philadelphia Black families including the Fortens, Purvis and White families and Ms# 339, The Resolution of the Benezet Joint Stock Association on the Death of Jacob C. White, Sr.", October, 1872 in The Leon Gardiner Collection, American Negro Historical Society Papers, Historical Society of Pennsylvania.

[3]George R. Prowell, The History of Camden County, NJ (Philadelphia: L.J. Richards Co, 1886), p. 709.

[4]Ibid.

United States Department of the Interior
National Park Service

National Register of Historic Places
Continuation Sheet

Section number ___8___   Page ___5___

THE PETER MOTT HOUSE
LAWNSIDE, CAMDEN COUNTY, NJ

The house is associated with the history of resistance,
individualism and achievement by blacks and whites in the abolition
movement. In spite of the harsh penalties provided against aiders
and abettors of runaways in the Fugitive Slave Law of 1850, Peter
Mott is said to have been actively involved in the effort to
promote freedom for members of his race trying to escape bondage.

Lawnside, an early nineteenth century African-American
community was first known as "Snow Hill", a name appearing in maps
as early as c. 1847[5]. The name may have been taken from Snow Hill,
Maryland, reputed to be the place of origin of many of its early
residents. In 1840 Ralph Smith, a white, Philadelphia abolitionist
gave to the residents land he owned along Warwick Road between the
present-day boroughs of Barrington and Haddonfield and designed a
formal village plan. He laid out lots[5] naming the locale "Free
Haven", to signify its role as a refuge from slavery. The lots were
sold at low prices to provide homesites for free blacks.

---

[5]See 83.90.405 "Map of the State of New Jersey within Ten
Miles of Philadelphia, c. 1847. Map Collection of the Camden County
Historical Society, Camden, NJ. Snow Hill is shown and identified
as "colored settlement".

[6]See 86.110.3.446. "A Tract of land at Snow Hill as laid in
lots and called Free Haven, then owned by Ralph Smith. William
Watson, esq., Surveyor, 1840. Map Collection of the Camden County
Historical Society, Camden, NJ.

United States Department of the Interior
National Park Service

National Register of Historic Places
Continuation Sheet

Section number ___8___ Page __6__

___

THE PETER MOTT HOUSE
LAWNSIDE, CAMDEN COUNTY, NJ

Smith may have been a Quaker with Haddonfield connections, cognizant of neighboring "Snow Hill". African-Americans had settled in the area long before Smith's efforts; he sought to develop the community and protect the property rights of those who had established new lives there.

In 1844 property adjacent to the Smith tract was purchased by Jacob C. White, Sr., a wealthy and influential Philadelphia African American dentist, from the estate of Dr. Bowman C. Hendry of Haddonfield, and added to the plan of Free Haven. Jacob White may have known Ralph Smith and been encouraged by him to acquire the land. The fact that White knew of the village is prima facie evidence that "Free Haven" played a role in White's anti-slavery activities. Lawnside's oral traditions have always included talk of the mix of free blacks, manumitted slaves (presumably of nearby Quakers) and runaways. In 1907 the village became known as "Lawnside"; the name had been used for the nearby Reading-Atlantic City Railroad station since 1883.

When the Philadelphia Vigilance Committee (PVC), the first organized society of the Underground Railroad, came into existence in 1838, Jacob C. White, Sr. was chosen as its Secretary. Financial support came from those who were sympathetic to its cause including White, William Still and Robert Purvis, all of whom were also actively engaged in its clandestine work. White's purchase of additional land for "Free Haven" came 6 years after the inception of the PVC giving weight to the statement made by the authors of The WPA Guide to 1930s New Jersey that the borough "...began as a station on the Underground Railroad."

___

[7]The WPA Guide to 1930s New Jersey, (New Brunswick, NJ: Rutgers University Press, Reprinted 1986). Compiled and written by the Federal Writers' project of the WPA for the State of NJ.

NPS Form 10-900-a
(8-86)

OMB Approval No. 1024-0018

United States Department of the Interior
National Park Service

National Register of Historic Places
Continuation Sheet

Section number ___8___   Page ___7___

THE PETER MOTT HOUSE
LAWNSIDE, CAMDEN COUNTY, NJ

In the 1840 census, Mott is listed as a free colored person between the ages of 24 and 36, employed in agriculture. A female in the same age category, probably Elizabeth Ann Thomas whom he married in New Jersey on November 2, 1833[8], was part of his household. Ten years later, in 1850, Mott was recorded as a 40 year-old laborer owning real estate valued at $600, born in New Jersey and unable to read or write. Eliza Ann Mott [sic] was also entered as illiterate and born in New Jersey.

The 1860 census reiterates the Motts' birthplace as New Jersey, indicates he is a farm worker owning real estate worth $200; however, the pair are not denoted "illiterate". In the 1870 enumeration, some years after the Civil War, Peter Mott, age 60 is a farmer with real estate valued at $1000. and a personal estate of $250., establishing him as one of the wealthier members of Free Haven. At this time, he and his wife, now called Ann are again classified as illiterate but Peter's birthplace is identified as Delaware and that of Ann as Virginia.

In 1880, at the last census taken during Mott's life time he was registered as a widowed plaster mason born in a slave state. He died the following year of "valvular heart disease" and is buried in Snow Hill Church (Mount Pisgah) Cemetery.

---

[8]Gloucester County Historical Society, Woodbury, NJ. The marriage was performed and recorded by Justice of the Peace, John Core.

121

NPS Form 10-900-a
(3-86)

OMB Approval No. 1024-0018

United States Department of the Interior
National Park Service

National Register of Historic Places
Continuation Sheet

Section number ____8____ Page __8____

THE PETER MOTT HOUSE
LAWNSIDE, CAMDEN COUNTY NJ

There can be no doubt that Mott was quite literate: his
signature appears on deeds he signed in 1850 and 1852; Elizabeth
Mott's signature, however, is represented by an "X". Mott's
important role in the community as a minister and Sunday School
official indicates that he was able to read. The contradctions may
be explained either by careless census-takers or Mott's reluctance
to admit he was a person of education from a slave state. Indeed,
since Mott's name does not appear in any New Jersey records until
his 1833 marriage, it is entirely possible that he, himself, was
one of the "contraband" led out of Delaware to freedom via the
Underground Railroad.

The history of this "transit system" is largely undocumented
even in the journals and writings of William Still, Robert Smedley
and Wilbur H. Siebert. It was a loosely connected system which
relied on the secrecy and commitment of those who participated.
"Conductors" and "agents" often appeared spontaneously; the work
was performed by volunteers acting according to their own
instincts; private homes served as "stations" and hiding places.
Few records were kept, many fugitives were illiterate. By the end
of the Civil War, the Underground Railroad ceased to function and
former operatives shifted their dedication to improving the status
of freed men; what we have learned about its system has largely
been acquired from written and oral accounts given at a later
date. Oral history in the black community provides a very strong
chain of evidence which cannot be discarded.

Miss Doris Scott, now in her late 70s, recalled, in a film
produced by Muneerah Higgs, _Lawnside: The Haven To Freedom_, her
grandmother telling her that Peter Mott used to take [fugitive]
slaves in his wagon to the Quakers in Haddonfield and Moorestown.
Miss Scott's grandmother, Mary Williams Bell (1850-1938) may have
been passing on information told her by her parents. Deeds and
maps in the possession of Miss Scott show that the Bell place
bordered the Mott property. Because of the proximity of their
homes, Mary Williams Bell undoubtedly knew Mott; in addition, her
family also attended Mount Pisgah Church before joining a break-
away congregation.

Wilbur H. Siebert, _The Underground Railroad From Slavery To
Freedom_. (New York: Russell & Russell, 1898, p. 11.

NPS Form 10-900-a
(8-86)

United States Department of the Interior
National Park Service

National Register of Historic Places
Continuation Sheet

OMB Approval No. 1024-0018

Section number ___8___ Page ___9___

THE PETER MOTT HOUSE
LAWNSIDE, CAMDEN COUNTY, NJ

Wilbur H. Siebert points out, "New Jersey was intimately associated with Philadelphia...in the underground system...from Philadelphia ...runaways were taken across the Delaware River to Camden...thence...to Burlington and...Bordentown." And, once a slave was led away to freedom, "... [he was] more likely to trust a black face...[because] a prominent feature of the Negro underground was providing of overnight accommodations..."[10]

New African American arrivals in Snow Hill in the years prior to the Civil War would never have caused suspicion and wariness; hospitality and warm welcome would have been awaiting them.

The Lawnside Historical Society which owns the Peter Mott House has been awarded $97,900. in matching funds from the NJ Historic Trust's Preservation Bond program because the significance of the Peter Mott House to the local community is so great that it is of the utmost importance to revitalize the building.

---

[10] Ibid., p. 123.

123

United States Department of the Interior
National Park Service

National Register of Historic Places
Continuation Sheet

Section number ___9___ Page __10__

PETER MOTT HOUSE
LAWNSIDE, CAMDEN COUNTY, NJ

BIBLIOGRAPHY

American Negro Historical Society Papers in the Leon Gardiner
    Collection, Historical Society of Pennsylvania.

Booker, Emmer H. 115th Anniversary of the Celebration and
    Rededication of the AME Mt. Pisgah CHurch.

Blockson, Charles H. The Underground Railroad in Pennsylvania,
    1981. North Carolina: Flame Press.

_____. "A Black Underground..." in Pennsylvania
    Heritage,IV,1.

Breyfogle, William. Make Free. NY: J.B. Lippincott, 1958.

Fairchild, James H., D.D. "The Underground Railroad" in Volume IV,
    Western Reserve Historical Society Tract #87.

Gopsil's Philadelphia Directory, 1870

McElroy's Philadelphia Directory.1839, 1840, 1841, 1842, 1843,
1852, 1857, 1861, 1865.

McGowan, James A. Station Master on the Underground Railroad.
    Pennsylvania: Whimsie Press, 1977.

Measday, Walter. Cape May and the Underground Railroad. n.d.

O'Brien's Philadelphia Directory, 1844, 1845, 1853.

Pennsylvania Abolition Society MS Collection, Vol. II. Historical
    Society of Pennsylvania.

PETER MOTT HOUSE
LAWNSIDE, CAMDEN COUNTY, NJ

BIBLIOGRAPHY (Continued)

The Philadelphia Colored Directory, 1907.

Prowell, George R. The History of Camden County, New Jersey.
        Philadelphia: L. J. Richards, Company, 1886.

Siebert, Wilbur H. The Underground Railroad from Slavery to
        Freedom. New York: Russell & Russell, 1898.

Smedley, R.C., M.D. A History of the Underground Railroad. 1883.

Spotts, C.D. The Pilgrim's Pathway. n.p.

Westfield Architects & Preservation Consultants. Feasibility Study
        of the Peter Mott House, 1991.

Peter Mott house   Camden County, NJ
Name of Property   County and State

10. Geographical Data

Acreage of Property __Less than 1 acre__

UTM References
(Place additional UTM references on a continuation sheet.)

1 | 1 8 | | 4 9 6 9 2 0 | | 4 4 1 2 8 2 0 |
  Zone   Easting   Northing

2 | | | | | | | | | | | | | | | |

3 | | | | | | | | | | | | | | | | |
  Zone   Easting   Northing

4 | | | | | | | | | | | | | | | |

☐ See continuation sheet

Verbal Boundary Description
(Describe the boundaries of the property on a continuation sheet.)

Boundary Justification
(Explain why the boundaries were selected on a continuation sheet.)

11. Form Prepared By

name/title __Gail Greenberg, County Historian__

organization __Camden County Cultural & Heritage Commission__ date __September 10, 1993__

street & number __250 South Park Drive__   telephone __(609) 858-0040__

city or town __Haddon Township__   state __NJ__   zip code __08108__

Additional Documentation
Submit the following items with the completed form:

Continuation Sheets

Maps

A **USGS map** (7.5 or 15 minute series) indicating the property's location.

A **Sketch map** for historic districts and properties having large acreage or numerous resources.

Photographs

Representative **black and white photographs** of the property.

Additional items
(Check with the SHPO or FPO for any additional items)

Property Owner
(Complete this item at the request of SHPO or FPO.)

name __Lawnside Historical Society__

street & number __P.O. Box 608__   telephone _____

city or town __Lawnside__   state __NJ__   zip code __08045__

Paperwork Reduction Act Statement: This information is being collected for applications to the National Register of Historic Places to nominate properties for listing or determine eligibility for listing, to list properties, and to amend existing listings. Response to this request is required to obtain a benefit in accordance with the National Historic Preservation Act, as amended (16 U.S.C. 470 et seq.)

126

THE PETER MOTT HOUSE
LAWNSIDE, CAMDEN COUNTY, N.J.

VERBAL BOUNDARY DESCRIPTION

    Block 44; Lot 19
    Lawnside Borough, Camden County, NJ

VERBAL BOUNDARY JUSTIFICATION

    The boundary includes the entire parcel containing the
Peter Mott House.

United States Department of the Interior
National Park Service

National Register of Historic Places
Continuation Sheet

Section number __CHAIN__   Page ___13___

THE PETER MOTT HOUSE, LAWNSIDE, NJ   CAMDEN COUNTY

CHAIN OF TITLE:

Date	Grantee	Grantor	Book/Page
		CAMDEN COUNTY REGISTER OF DEEDS	
2/20/92	Lawnside Historical So.	Narberth Dev. Corp.	4543/470
7/25/90	Narberth Dev. Corp.	Estate/Pearl Faulcon	4452/352
12/9/63	Pearl Faulcon	Mary E. Clayton	3939/216
10/31/41	Chas. Clayton	Joseph E. Moore	1159/295
9/4/1895	Joseph E. Moore	Lewis [Levis] Moore	207/619
6/21/1879	Lewis[Levis] Moore	Peter Mott	94/623
3/3/1849	Peter Mott (part A)	L. Phifer, Esq.	I/22
5/30/1844	Peter Mott (part B)	Thos. Stephenson	I/30
10/10/1850	Peter Mott (part C)	Jacob C. White	N/305
		GLOUCESTER COUNTY REGISTER OF DEEDS	
A: 10/3/1808	Stephen Thomas	Thos. Stephenson	M.295
B: 7/15/1806	Thos. Stephenson	Jacob Jennings (Lot #6)	None
1/15/1806	Thos. Stephenson	Jacob Jennings (Lot #5	M.295
C: 9/23/1844	Jacob C. White	Estate/Dr. Bowman C. Hendry	B/352
11/18/1813	Dr. Bowman C. Hendry	Isaac Burrough	BB/371
1/15/1806	Isaac Burrough	Jacob Jennings	None

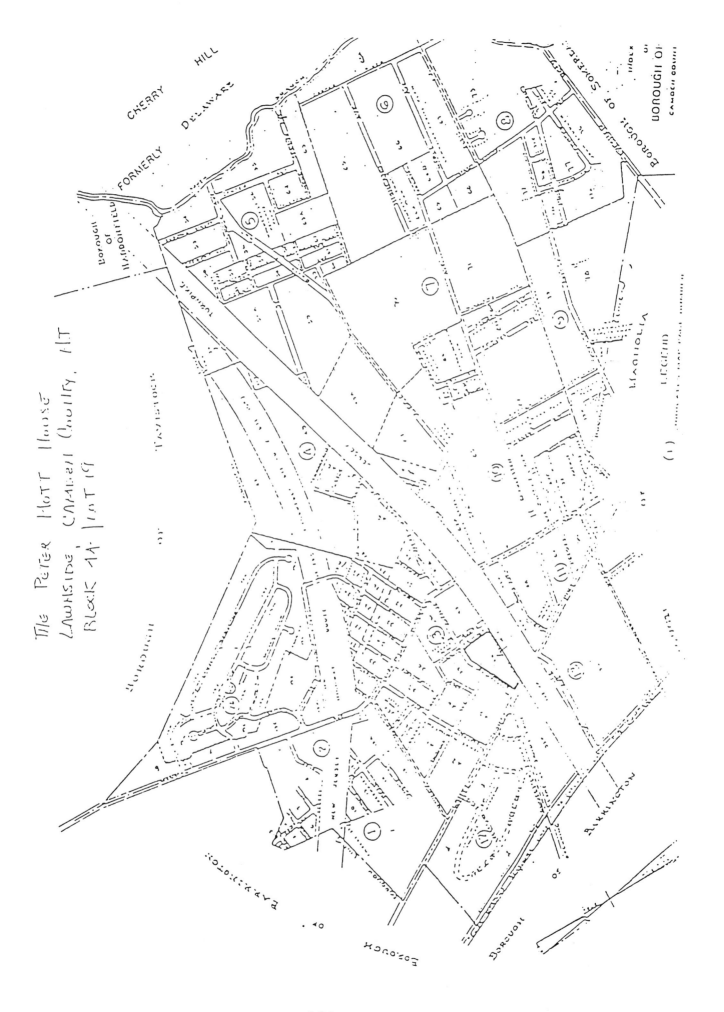

The Peter Mott House
Lawnside Camden County, NJ
Block 44, Lot 19

CHERRY HILL

FORMERLY DELAWARE

BOROUGH OF HADDONFIELD

BOROUGH OF SOMERDALE

BOROUGH OF

BOROUGH OF

BOROUGH OF

BARRINGTON

LEGEND

129

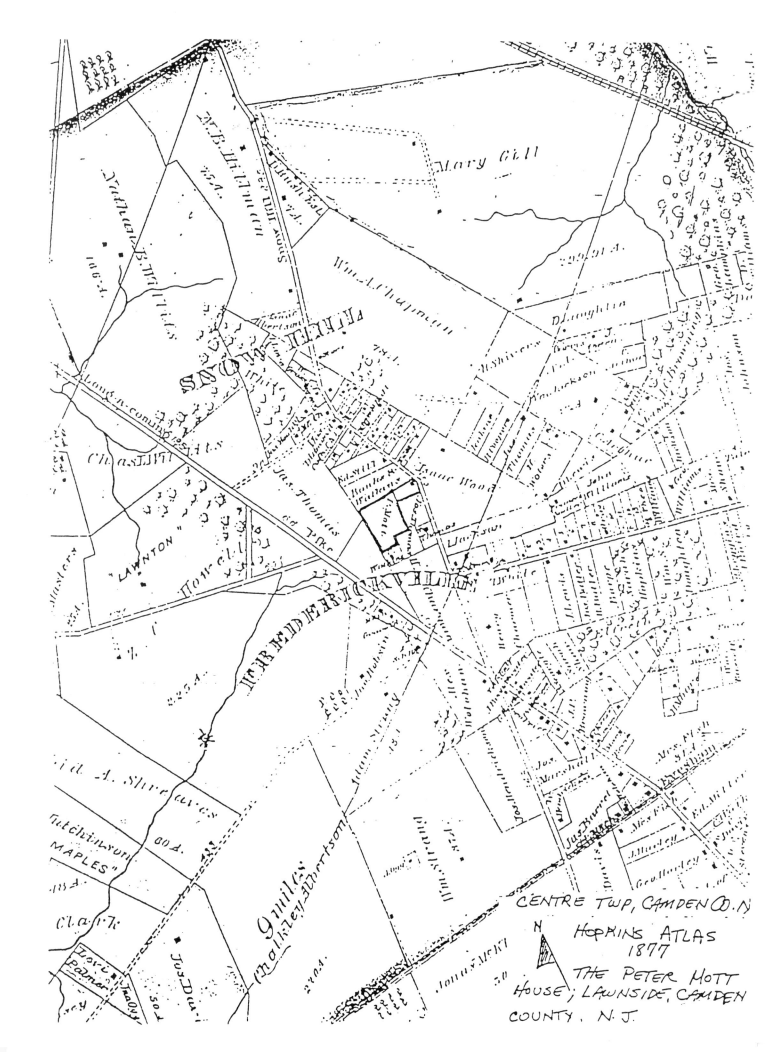

CENTRE TWP, CAMDEN CO. N.

HOPKINS ATLAS
1877

THE PETER MOTT
HOUSE, LAWNSIDE, CAMDEN
COUNTY, N.J.

United States Department of the Interior
National Park Service

National Register of Historic Places
Continuation Sheet

Section number <u>PHOTOS</u> Page <u>14</u>

Peter Mott House
Lawnside, Camden County, New Jersey

PHOTOGRAPHS

The following is the same for all photographs:

1.) Peter Mott House

2.) Camden County, New Jersey

3.) Martin Shore, Photographer

4.) April, 1992

5.) Negatives held by Margaret Westfield, R.A.
   Westfield Architects & Preservation Consultants
   425 White Horse Pike
   Haddon Heights, NJ 08035
   (609) 547-0465

6.) View of Peter Mott House, looking southwest
7.) Photograph 1 of 7

6.) View of north and east elevations, looking southwest
7.) Photograph 2 of 7

6.) View of south and west elevations, looking northeast
7.) Photograph 3 of 7

6.) Interior view of first floor northern room, looking southwest
7.) Photograph 4 of 7

Photo 1

PETER MOTT HOUSE, CAMDEN COUNTY N.J., PHOTO # 1

PETER MOTT HOUSE, CAMDEN COUNTY N.J. PHOTO # 2

Photo 2

Photo 3

Photo 4

PETER MOTT HOUSE, CAMDEN COUNTY N.J., PHOTO # 3

PETER MOTT HOUSE, CAMDEN COUNTY, N.J. PHOTO #4

These photographs have been reduced for the purposes of this book. Photos submitted with the NRHP application should be black and white, preferably 8' X 10" with borders and unmounted. The smallest acceptable size is 3 1/2" X 5" See Page 73 for detailed instructions.

THE PETER MOTT HOUSE
LAWNSIDE, CAMDEN Co., NJ

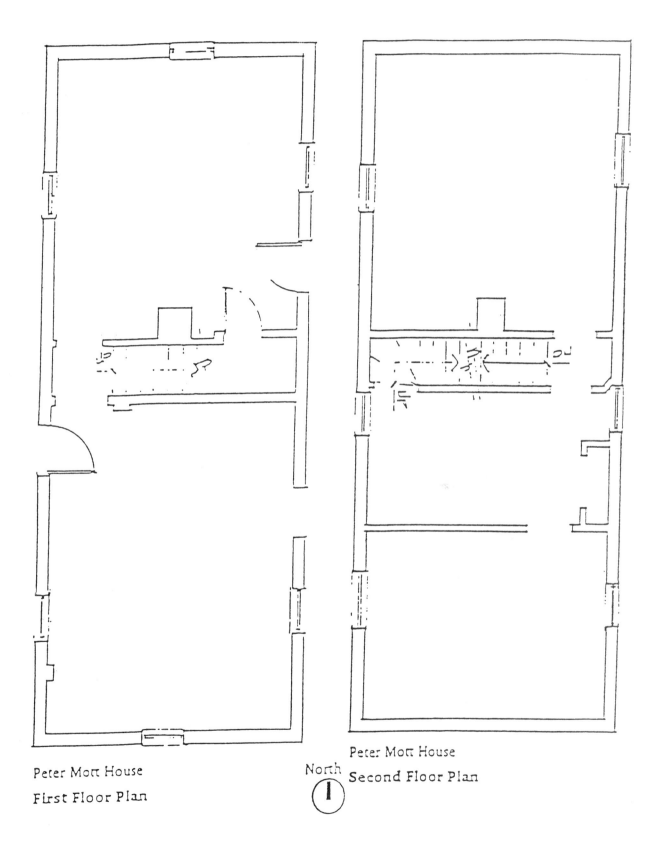

Peter Mott House

First Floor Plan

North

Peter Mott House

Second Floor Plan

INdEX